Praise for *The Reading Zone*

"If students in Nancie Atwell's reading zone are 'joyfully literate,' then readers of her book will become delirious with joy as they are immersed into a classroom of serious readers. Atwell and her students demonstrate how the act of reading itself transcends the national rhetoric about scientific reading instruction."

—ReLEAH COSSETT LENT, author of *Engaging Adolescent Learners*

"Nancie allows us to listen to classroom conversations around books and reading. She allows us to witness wise teaching and shows us how to take children into books and help them live among the characters, to experience along with the author, and to construct a personally relevant understanding through passionate participation with the text. She reminds us that we, educators, are the ones who have the knowledge to take children on this journey. Join me in a call for a return to common sense in our classrooms. Let Nancie lead the way."

—LESTER LAMINACK, author of *Learning Under the Influence of Language and Literature: Making the Most of Read-Alouds Across the Day*

"I love that Nancie is open and honest about her own learning, thinking and changing over her years as a teacher of reading. She is there in the classroom with her students, figuring out how best to support her young readers; her role as a teacher is critical to the success of her reading workshop. She shares what it takes to be the kind of teacher who can invite kids into the world of reading, not just for school, but for a lifetime."

—FRANKI SIBBERSON, author of *Beyond Leveled Books* and *Still Learning to Read*, intermediate multiage teacher, Dublin City Schools, Ohio

"In an era of reading instruction characterized by strategies and comprehension tests and words per minute, Nancie Atwell goes to the heart of the reading experience. Through vivid examples, she shows us how we can help our students enter the 'reading zone' and revel in the simple but profound power of a child lost in a book."

—MAJA WILSON, author of *Rethinking Rubrics*, high school English teacher, Ludington, Michigan

"Building on intimacy with the books that might interest her students, Nancie Atwell presents a much-needed vision of how to connect kids and books. There are no worksheets, no projects, and no gimmicks to interfere with what counts—students making choices and learning to read for pleasure. Atwell provides a passionate guide for assessing students' growth in ways that match what readers do. *The Reading Zone* is where we all need to be."

—SUSAN OHANIAN, author of *Caught in the Middle: Nonstandard Children* and *A Killing Curriculum*

"Nancie Atwell brilliantly plunges us into the heart of reading, and shows through her lived classroom experience how to take kids there. Passionate, proficient readers develop not through programs but through a rich reading community and daily immersion in the 'reading zone.'"

—SANDRA WILDE, author of *Spelling Strategies and Patterns*, Professor, Portland State University

"Nancie Atwell never fails to inspire or to tell it like it is. In *The Reading Zone*, she lays out in no uncertain terms what could, should, and ought to be happening in every reading classroom, in every school in our nation. Her rich narrative provides hope and ammunition to experienced teachers who want to bring books and kids together in meaningful ways. For new teachers, *The Reading Zone* is certain to spark the imagination, providing a vision for the kind of classroom that is possible when kids and teachers work together with the shared goal of creating skilled, passionate, habitual, critical readers."

—KAREN SMITH, Professor, Arizona State University

"*The Reading Zone* takes the ground-breaking work of *In the Middle* and raises the stakes. Atwell's clarion call to action not only provides educators with the rationale for implementing reading workshop, *The Reading Zone* explodes the myths and rebuffs the attacks leveled against it in this age of NCLB. Atwell's passion for kids, books, and reading shines through on every page of this remarkable book."

—TERI LESESNE, author of *Making the Match: The Right Book for the Right Reader at the Right Time* and *Naked Reading!*

*For Toby, who taught me what it means
to make of reading a personal art.*

Acknowledgments

Many others had a hand in *The Reading Zone*. I'm grateful first to the friends and educators who read and responded to drafts at critical junctures: my heartfelt thanks to Gerald Bracey, Carole Edelsky, Elaine Garan, Gloria Pipkin, and Sandra Wilde for clarifications, advice, and encouragement.

Special thanks go to the extraordinary reading teachers of the Center for Teaching and Learning (CTL). Helene Coffin, Ted DeMille, Jill Cotta, and Glenn Powers are four of my teaching heroes—and personal artists beyond compare.

I'm also grateful to Joanna Davis-Swing, production manager of this book, for her smart, engaged, efficient coordination of its publication; to Maria Lilja, who designed the elegant layout; and to John Gayle, Mike Gibbons, and Roberta Jordan for photographs that show CTL readers immersed in the zone.

Finally, *The Reading Zone* exists because of Lois Bridges and Toby McLeod. Lois's responses as an editor are a writer's dream. They fuel my thinking, fill my heart to the brim, and send me straight back to my desk. Her commitment to children, teachers, literacy, and justice is unwavering. Toby, my husband, took hundreds of pages of hatched-up, crossed-out, handwritten drafts and turned them into a beautiful manuscript. I owe these two for their sharp insights, superb editorial assistance, continuous cheerleading, and time immeasurable.

The days that make us happy
make us wise.

—JOHN MASEFIELD

Table of Contents

Foreword

The writer Nora Ephron suggests that "There's something called the rapture of the deep, and it refers to what happens when a deep-sea diver spends too much time at the bottom of the ocean and can't tell which way is up. When he resurfaces, he's liable to have a condition called the bends, where the body can't adapt to the oxygen levels in the atmosphere. All this happens to me when I resurface from a book."

Nancie Atwell's book, *The Reading Zone: How to Help Kids Become Skilled, Passionate, Habitual, Critical Readers*, made me feel the rapture of the deep. With eloquence and honesty, she reminds us of just how remarkable a room filled with young readers can be. With beautifully crafted classroom scenes, student work samples, and paragraphs packed with sensible teaching suggestions, Nancie reminds us of what's important in the teaching of reading, freeing literacy teachers to abandon the fads and formulas that have spread like wildfire through our reading workshops. More important, she offers expert, practical, and oh such sane advice for inviting students to feel the rapture of the deep, to enter their own Reading Zones, becoming the kind of readers we all envy.

With the publication of this bold and courageous book, Nancie Atwell is putting two hands on our shoulders, demanding that we take back our literacy classrooms. I easily envision *The Reading Zone* becoming the centerpiece of staff room conversations, challenging literacy educators to rethink their reading goals, redefine their practice, and reestablish their own reading lives.

—Shelley Harwayne

CHAPTER 1

The Personal Art

A second-grade reader and personal artist

It's a morning in November. Outside the sky has already turned the peculiar yellow-grey of winter in Maine. Inside my classroom, under banks of fluorescent lights, seventh and eighth graders lie sprawled on beanbag chairs. They're decked out in the current uniform of American adolescence: jeans ripped at the knees on purpose, logo T-shirts, hoodies. I've just finished scooting among them and whispering a conversation with each boy and girl: "How is it?" or "What do you think so far?" or "What's happening now?" and, always, "What page are you on?" Now I'm back in my rocking chair. Except for the turning of pages, the room is still.

If you had observed these students on any other occasion in their waking lives—say, yesterday at recess as they shot hoops, exchanged iPods, teased, and screamed—it might be hard to reconcile that noise with this quiet. But here, in reading workshop, it's dead silent because my kids are gone. Each boy and girl has vanished into an invisible world. Each, as they put it, is lost in the reading zone.

Nineteen students are reading nineteen books. Nate, an eighth grader, is deep into Dalton Trumbo's antiwar classic *Johnny Got His Gun*, which I extolled in a booktalk along with Vonnegut's *Slaughterhouse-Five*, *Fallen Angels* by Walter Dean Myers, and Tim O'Brien's *The Things They Carried*. Nate's friend Lincoln finished the O'Brien yesterday and rated it a 9 out of 10; now, at his mom's suggestion, he's trying *Huckleberry Finn*. Charlotte and Anna are getting their feet wet in memoir—*Girl, Interrupted* and *The Glass Castle,* respectively. Chloe the dog lover is invisible behind *Marley and Me*, a title Anna booktalked to the class last week, and Phoebe barely breathes as she nears the end of *I Am Not Esther* by Fleur Beale. Hayley, an eighth grader, says she loves *The Girls' Guide to Hunting and Fishing*. I flash back to last fall, when fantasy was her exclusive diet, because today Henry, a seventh grader, is caught up in Zizou Corder's *Lionboy*, the first volume in a fantasy trilogy that Hayley taught me about a year ago and urged me to buy for our library. Alex, another seventh-grade guy, has lost himself in the third volume, *Lionboy: The Truth*.

Wyatt is taking a break from Stephen King, he says, with Robert McCammon's *Boy's Life*, a novel I touted to him as King for kids and a 10-plus. Next to Wyatt, Nathaniel shakes he is laughing so hard at something in *Dave Barry Slept Here*. Grace, who surprised herself with how much she liked the new film version of *Pride and Prejudice*, is happily surprising herself with Austen; I told her that's how I came to Austen, too, but via Greer Garson and Laurence Olivier. Rose's black fingernails grip a vampire novel by Amelia Atwater-Rhodes, and at her side, Tess is nearing the surprise ending of Pete Hautman's *Invisible*—I can tell because she caught my eye and mouthed the words *Oh my God. I know*, I mouth back. Cam B., eighth-grade sports maven, reads a new novel by John Coy. Last spring he wrote an essay about steroid abuse in the major leagues, so when I was browsing Borders and found *Crackback*, about a high school athlete pressured to use steroids, I bought it for Cam and asked if he wanted to preview it for the group. He's fifty pages in and says it's already at least a 9. His bud, Cam L., is inhaling Terry Trueman's page-turner *Stuck in Neutral*. And Sophie, who abandoned two novels in quick succession last week, grabbed Meg Cabot's *Avalon High* after I booktalked it today, mostly for Sophie's benefit. So far, she says, so good.

When I look up from my book and notice the time, I tell them, "As you're ready, find a stopping place, mark your page, and come up for air." One by one they segue from the stories they've been living back into the here and now. They yawn and stretch—it can take a physical effort to cross the boundary. And then they're fully themselves again. They yammer at me and one another about their books, overstuff their backpacks, forget to put away the beanbags, and slam out of the room to their next class. Tonight they'll read for at least half an hour—that's everyone's homework every night. Tomorrow in school they'll read some more— the next day, too. By June each boy and girl will have finished at least thirty books; a few will read and record more than one hundred titles.

Over my twenty years of teaching reading in a workshop, the annual average for a class of seventh and eighth graders is at least forty titles. In the lower grades at our school, the Center for Teaching and Learning (CTL), the numbers are similarly remarkable. The K–6 teachers and I make time every day for our students to curl up with good books and engage in the single activity that consistently correlates with high levels of performance on standardized tests of reading ability. And that is *frequent, voluminous reading*. A child sitting in a quiet room with a good book isn't a flashy or, more significantly, marketable teaching method. It just happens to be the only way anyone ever grew up to become a reader.

And that is the goal: for every child to become a skilled, passionate, habitual, critical reader—as novelist Robertson Davies put it, to learn how to make of reading "a personal art." Along the way, CTL teachers hope our students will become smarter, happier, more just, and more compassionate people because of the worlds they experience within those hundreds of thousands of black lines of print.

We know that students need time to read, at school and at home, every day. And we understand that when particular children love their particular books, reading is more likely to happen during the time we set aside for it. The only surefire way to induce a love of books is to invite students to select their own.

So CTL teachers help children to choose books, develop and refine their literary criteria, and carve out identities for themselves as readers. We *get* that it's essential that every child we teach be able to say, "These are my favorite authors, genres, books, and characters this year, and this is why." Personal preference is the foundation for anyone who will make of reading a personal art.

Starting in kindergarten and going straight through until the end of high school, free choice of books should be a young reader's right, not a privilege granted by a kind teacher. Our students have shown us that opportunities to consider, select, and reconsider books make reading feel sensible and attractive to children right from the start—and that they will read more books than we ever dreamed possible and more challenging books than we ever dreamed of assigning to them.

A sixth-grade reader lost in her favorite genre—fantasy

We've learned, too, that students need access to a generous assortment of inviting titles. Instead of investing in class sets of expensive basals and anthologies, our school makes classroom collections of individual titles the budget priority. No child ever grew to become a skilled, passionate, habitual, critical reader via a fat, bland textbook.

And we learned that we need to read a lot of the books we hope our students will, so we can make knowledgeable recommendations, offer help when readers get stuck, and teach children one at a time about books and reading in the daily, quiet conversations of our workshops.

Finally, CTL's reading teachers have learned that the only delivery system for reading comprehension is reading. When reading is meaningful, understanding cannot be separated from decoding. Comprehension isn't a set of sub-skills children have to be taught to bring to bear after they have translated letters to sounds. When kids are reading stories that are interesting to them, when the books are written at their independent reading levels, comprehension—the making of meaning—is direct, and the kids *understand*.

Human beings are wired to understand. As reading theorist Frank Smith put it, "Children know how to comprehend, provided they are in a situation that has the possibility of making sense to them" (1997). Reading workshop is our best approximation of an instructional context that has the possibility of making sense to young readers. A child sits in a quiet room with a beloved, accessible book, in the company of classmates who are reading and loving books, too, and a teacher who knows about literature, reading, and his or her students—as readers and as people.

This is not a dream world. Because CTL is a nonprofit demonstration school—a place that public school teachers come to learn about good teaching—we handpick a student body that represents a diverse range of socioeconomic backgrounds and ability levels. I raise money twelve months a year so that we can set the tuition rate as low as possible—most recently, $4,800 per year, with a third of families receiving additional tuition assistance. The point is to attract a mix of students in whom visiting teachers can recognize their own.

And they do, because CTL students are regular kids. They suffer ADHD, depression, and identified learning disabilities, including nonverbal learning disorders, visual-processing difficulties, and dyslexia. Some kids come from homes with packed bookshelves; some own only a few books of their own. Maine is a rural state and a poor one, in the bottom third in terms of per capita income. Only 66 percent of jobs here pay a livable wage, and our students' parents work hard at all kinds of occupations: farmer, carpenter, sheetrocker, store clerk, soldier, fisherman, gardener, postal worker, and housecleaner, as well as physician, minister, teacher, executive, and small-business owner.

So how and what our students read can't be explained away as an anomaly. This is not a privileged population of students. This is what is possible for children as readers.

Which leads to the obvious question. If educators can agree that a goal of education is for children to become skilled, passionate, habitual, critical readers, why does so much of what goes on in the name of teaching reading *prevent* such reading from happening? The sheer waste of children's time, day in and year out, is mind-numbing, as teachers and administrators fall prey to the latest spate of faulty research, instructional franchises, and textbook-company promises that lead to practices that are questionable at best and, at worst, damage children as readers. Yet, every day, well-meaning teachers erect instructional roadblocks between their students and the pure *pleasure* of the personal art.

And there it is: the P word. I know, because I've felt it, too, that there's a sense of uneasiness among teachers and parents about an approach like reading work-shop. Shouldn't there be some pedagogic strings attached here? Some paper-and-pencil and small-group activities that look like schoolwork? Because otherwise, isn't reading class, well, too enjoyable?

We need to get over it. When teachers embrace our role as literate grown-ups who invite students to enter, again and again, one of the most pleasurable experiences that human existence has to offer, then our students will embrace books and reading. This is a noble endeavor. This is more than enough for society to ask of teachers, or for teachers to ask of kids. To quote Robertson Davies again, the goal is "to read for pleasure, but not for idleness; for pastime but not to kill time; to seek, and find, delight and enlargement of life in books" (1959). This sounds to me like language for a job description: *Wanted: A teacher who can help children seek, and find, delight and enlargement of life in books.*

But open the door of an American elementary classroom during reading time, or a high school English class at any time, in search of the authentic pleasures of the reading life. What you're likely to find are teachers talking and children listening, making notes, filling in blanks, discussing in groups, writing reports, studying vocabulary—everything but reading a good book.

An American poet who consistently captures the admiration of my seventh- and eighth-grade boys is William Stafford. They often name his sly "Notice What This Poem Is Not Doing" as a favorite. Consider for a moment the nonsense that passes for reading instruction in our schools by noticing what teaching reading in a workshop is *not* doing.

First, it's not telling kids they aren't smart or trustworthy enough to choose books and determine which ones are good and right for them. As Virginia Woolf observed, "Literature is no one's private ground, literature is common ground; let us trespass freely and fearlessly and find our own way for ourselves." A reading workshop takes down the Keep Off the Grass signs. It invites young readers to

A fifth- and sixth-grade reading workshop

explore and enjoy the lushest landscapes on earth, and, through booktalks and one-to-one conversations, it recommends the worthwhile, scenic routes.

Also notice how reading workshop doesn't impede the journey or exact a toll. There are no tests, worksheets, self-sticking notes, projects, book reports, double-entry journals, or discussion questions between the last page of one good book and the first page of the next. Teachers who help kids act as readers learn how to assess their growth in ways that match what readers do: in a nutshell, the teachers talk with young readers, and they listen to them.

Notice that there aren't any rewards for all this reading. The principal doesn't dye her hair green or host an ice-cream party when the student body reads a million words. In reading workshop, the delights are intrinsic, always: *This week I got to experience a whole world with characters I loved; inside me I traveled, wondered, worried, laughed, cried, raged, triumphed.* The passions aroused by stories and characters are the prize.

Notice that reading as a personal art doesn't contort or clutter the landscape with "reading activities." There isn't a worksheet, vocabulary building exercise, discussion group, bulletin board display, or metacognitive strategy session in sight. But there are booktalks, read-alouds, conversations, time, silence, comfort, simple systems of record keeping, and a classroom library that gets bigger and better every year, because teachers understand that volume of reading and enthusiasm for reading are keys, and everything else is either a frill or a boondoggle.

Notice that reading workshop teachers don't give kids misinformation about reading—or outright bad advice. Here children are encouraged to skim, skip, and look ahead. Abandoning a book that a reader isn't enjoying is viewed as a smart move, not a character defect. Study skills aren't confused with the aesthetic act of living in a good story, and readers of fiction aren't instructed to activate the schemas of proficient readers. No one tells children they have to record and look up unfamiliar vocabulary. No one judges a child's fluency based on his or her proficiency at reading aloud cold. And reading workshop teachers *get* rereading. They know that the desire to reenter a beloved book isn't cheating; it's a benchmark of someone who is becoming a personal artist.

The reading teacher's goal should be to eliminate—or at least reduce—frustration and to *make reading easy.* We start by being honest with kids about what we do as readers. We understand that most of the act of reading stories—the best part—lies below the level of consciousness and belongs there, as we're swept along in an indescribable stream of images and impressions. So reading workshop teachers forgo methods that interrupt the flow. And we acknowledge the guilt that many of us grew up with—the feeling that there's a proper, rigorous way to read and that somehow we're not doing it right—so we can help our students navigate books with pleasure and confidence.

And notice how reading workshop is not stereotyping boys. Reading workshop teachers haven't jumped on the bandwagon that decided reading is an activity better suited to girls because it's passive, unpractical, and cerebral. Instead, we talk to our guys, listen to them, and prowl bookstores. We find the stories and characters that boys will love, deliver our best sales pitches, and put books and time in boys' hands. We've learned that choice of books is of the utmost importance for young male readers, and that the only gender difference that matters is that girls tend to be able to find books on their own. Guys need adult help—teachers and parents who make it our business to keep an eye out for good stories for the boys in our lives.

Finally, notice that reading workshop is not S.S.R. It's not a study hall, where we watch the clock with one eye as we Drop Everything And Read. Teachers in a reading workshop are creating readers for a lifetime. We introduce new books and old favorites, tell about authors and genres, read aloud authors and genres, and talk with kids about their reading rituals and plans. We teach the elements of fiction; how poems work; what efficient readers do—and don't do—when they come across an unfamiliar word; how punctuation gives voice to reading; when to speed up or slow down; who won this year's Newbery Award; how to keep useful reading records; what a sequel is; what readers can glean from a copyright page; how to identify the narrative voice or tone of a novel and why it matters; that there are different purposes for reading that affect a reader's style and pace; how to identify a beach book or page-turner; how to tell if a book is too hard, too easy, or just right; and why the only way to become a strong, fluent reader is to read often and a lot.

If it's not obvious by now, this book is nothing less than a manifesto. Here is my evidence, gathered over twenty years of working directly and successfully with all kinds of kids, that it's reading that makes readers. Frequent, voluminous, happy experiences with books—preferably in a room that's filled with good ones and in the company of a teacher who knows how to invite and sustain a love of stories—are the way to teach and learn reading for a lifetime.

As a classroom teacher, reading workshop is one of the simplest and hardest things I do. It's also the most worthwhile. Our students leave CTL as strong, literary, well-above-grade-level readers. But they also leave *smarter*, about such a diversity of words, ideas, events, artifacts, people, and places that they can take my breath away. Books bring the whole world to a tiny school in rural Maine. And then the children grow up, leave the school, and recognize the wide world they encounter out there because it is already lodged in the "chambers of their imaginations" (Spufford, 2002).

Sydney Jourard wrote, "The vicarious experience of reading can shape our essence, change us, just as firsthand experience can. Experience seems to be as transfusible as blood" (1971). For kids who know reading as a personal art, every day is a transfusion. Every day they engage with literature that enables them to know things, feel things, imagine things, hope for things, become people they never could have dreamed without the transforming power of books, books, books.

High on a wall of my classroom hangs a poster I made years ago. It's a quotation from Dylan Thomas: "My proper education consisted of the liberty to read whatever I cared to. I read indiscriminately and all the time, with my eyes hanging out . . ." When I gaze out from my rocking chair each day over that sea of beanbags, ripped denim, and adolescents reading with their eyes hanging out, I recognize education at its best. The room is still and silent because it has to be. Readers' minds are learning to form the questions that are worth asking and filling up with the knowledge of the world.

CHAPTER 2

Reading in the Zone

Middle schoolers immersed in the reading zone

Some of my students enter our school as kindergartners and begin to choose, read, and love books as five-year-olds. About half join us along the way, a few as late as grade eight. Every September, when students come together to form the new seventh- and eighth-grade class, they represent a spectrum of middle-school readers—different tastes, attitudes, abilities, and prior experiences. But by November, their common denominator as readers is that everyone easily and regularly enters *the zone.*

Jed, a seventh grader, coined the phrase. It was his interpretation of the condition Thomas Newkirk characterized, in a journal article, as "the reading state" (2000). Newkirk expressed his concern about kids who don't love reading because they've never experienced the intense involvement, the "heightened form of pleasure," that readers of books find ourselves in all the time.

I gave my students copies of Newkirk's article because I was curious about their take on it. It seemed to me that an inability or lack of desire to enter the reading state wasn't an issue for the boys and girls at our school. By Thanksgiving of any year, teachers of grades 1–8 could practically snap our fingers like hypnotists at the start of reading workshop, and every kid would be *there.* But why?

So I asked the seventh and eighth graders to think about three questions: Do you understand what Newkirk means by the reading state? If so, what's it like for you? And, if so, what are the conditions at CTL that make it possible for you to enter a state of engagement as a reader and stay there?

First, yes, every student, including those with reading difficulties, recognized what was meant by "the reading state." When Jed said it was more of a zone than a state, the phrase stuck. Individuals' answers to the second question defined the zone: the place readers went when they left our classroom behind and lived vicariously in their books.

Three quarters of the kids compared the zone to a private, internal movie, *but better.* Nick, one of the stronger readers, wrote: "First of all, you see what's happening in your head, like a movie screen. You care about the characters and think about what you would do at every point where they make a decision. You block out the sounds of the outside world. Eventually, it doesn't even feel like you're reading. You don't seem to be actually reading the words as much as it's just happening. And last, you don't want to stop reading."

Michael, a struggling reader, agreed: "When I'm in my reading zone, I feel like I'm a character in the book I'm reading. When I'm in my reading zone, it's almost like a TV show or a movie. I can see it really well. I can feel, taste, see, smell when I'm in my reading zone. Everything around you disappears and all you care about are the characters."

Empathy plays a significant role in the zone. Students wrote about placing themselves in relation to the characters in stories, something that seemed to happen unconsciously and automatically. Tyler wrote, "It's hard to explain. It's like you're in the book, like right next to the main character, but you're thinking his thoughts." Audrey noted, "First, I have to be in a great book. Otherwise I don't want to enter it. But once I do, I don't always become the main character. Sometimes I become a best friend of the main character, someone who doesn't talk but just listens to his or her problems and joys. I feel as if the character needs me there, so I don't want to leave the novel." Forrest articulated a system for casting his mental movie: "Right away, literally the second I start reading the first line, I begin formulating the 'movie' of the book. With girl characters, I am watching the 'movie,' but with boy characters, I am the star."

Many students described almost a fugue state when absorbed in a book: "I forget where I am and who's around me and even who I am." "You don't notice that you're turning pages or going on to the next chapter." "You're not aware of the page number or what technique the author used or what the theme is." "Time goes by incredibly fast, but I'm not aware of it at all." "You get lost, but in a good way." For rapt readers, comprehension has everything to do with being lost in the zone.

Finally, each student described the school conditions that make this level of absorption possible. Forrest, a seventh grader who had been at our school for six months, wrote that in order to enter the reading zone, he discovered he needed:

- *encouragement from the teacher, and advice;*
- *time to read at school;*
- *trillions of great books as backups;*
- *silence, absolute silence, to help be transported into "The World";*
- *booktalks to recommend great books;*
- *comfortable cushions and pillows; and*
- *a healthy chunk of time (thirty minutes) to read at home every night.*

I categorized all their responses—what the group perceived as essential if a reading class was to be transformed into a reading zone. In the order in which they were most mentioned, the following are the top ten school conditions my students said make engaged reading possible, not to mention likely.

1. Booktalks and mini-lessons (cited by 88 percent of respondents)

2. A big, diverse classroom library with regular new additions (74 percent)

3. Quiet, daily, in-class time to read (73 percent)

4. Individuals' free choice of books, authors, and genres (56 percent)

5. Recommendations of books from friends and the teacher and a special bookshelf for kids' favorites (54 percent)

6. Comfort during in-class reading time (53 percent)

7. Students' letters to the teacher and friends about their reading (53 percent)

8. Individuals' conversations with the teacher about their reading (31 percent)

9. Individuals' lists of the books they want to read someday (30 percent)

10. Homework reading of at least half an hour every night (30 percent)

A condition I felt special gratitude for was the kids' acknowledgment of a reader's need for quiet. After twenty years, I still suffer twinges of guilt when I have to ask students to stop talking during reading workshop. *But they're talking about books! They're socializing about literature!* And they're not reading. And they're distracting the readers around them. And if I don't remind them about the silence rule, I'm giving everyone else permission to stop reading and start talking, too.

So it's quiet during the workshop. But when the reading is rich, the reading environment extends on its own beyond the classroom and the schedule. Students who immerse themselves in the zone find plenty of opportunities after they emerge from it to talk with their friends about books they love, just as I do in my life as a reader, just as you do in yours.

If the sounds of speech during reading are a distraction, so is music, even classical compositions. For some children, any noise makes absorption difficult. This includes the noise a teacher makes. When my students are reading and I move among them to chat about their books, I whisper. Readers whisper in response.

A first- and second-grade reading workshop

In September, I teach a lesson about quiet during reading workshop as an act of thoughtfulness, in all the senses of the word. And the first week I ask the group, at the end of independent reading time, to talk about how hard or easy it was to enter the zone in a room filled with others. Speaking for myself, it takes about four reading workshops each September to feel comfortable reading in a group again, even a quiet, thoughtful one.

Young readers find that psychological comfort is easier to achieve when they're physically comfortable; hence the vinyl-covered beanbags and whistle cushions that my students sprawl on as they read. At a school where I previously taught, the principal was irked no end by the sight of adolescent readers sprawling. It offended his sense of decorum. So I learned to spare him by covering the window in the classroom door with a sign: DO NOT DISTURB. READERS AT WORK. And even with their feet up and their heads down, they were.

I was surprised when almost a third of the kids mentioned nightly reading as a condition essential to their presence in the zone. It must have pained them to have to admit any benefit to homework. But given the constraints of a middle school schedule, I can't make enough time during class for students to become skilled, passionate, habitual, critical readers. After each day's poem, mini-lesson, and time for independent writing, they get about twenty minutes in the zone: not as generous as I'd like, but enough time to engage and, I hope, to understand that reading is one of the priorities in this classroom and their lifetimes and should be carried on at home as well.

The baseline homework, the most important assignment any teacher can give is reading. At CTL, we ask students to take their books home with them every afternoon, read for at least half an hour, and bring the books back the next morning. When I circulate among readers during the workshop, one of my whispered queries is, "What page are you on?" I record the title and page number on a form

I carry on a clipboard. With few exceptions, a student who isn't at least 20 pages beyond yesterday is in homework trouble.

Every student begins the year with a homework pass in each subject: one time when a teacher will excuse uncompleted work. After that, for each missing assignment, I mail home a computerized letter to parents that explains what wasn't done and asks for their involvement. After three letters, I schedule a meeting with the student and his or her parents to discuss how we can work together to help the child come to school prepared.

When the missing schoolwork is the nightly half-hour of reading, the focus of the conference is on *why*: Is there no obvious place at home for the child to read? No obvious time? Is the student forgetting to take home his or her book? Do the parents and child understand how important frequent, voluminous reading is to his or her future, as a student and a human being?

I am not hoping that frequent, voluminous reading will happen. I am using everything I know about books and every system I can invent to make sure it does, starting with students' free choice of great stories and ending with homework letters and parent conferences when a child is having a hard time developing the reading habit and taking the zone home.

The remaining conditions for engaged reading named by my students deserve ample time and space. Choice, booktalks, oral and written conversations about books, and the logistics of teaching reading in a workshop are topics still to come in greater depth.

In looking back at the big picture of what my students said compels them to enter the reading zone and stay there, what's most striking to me about the top ten conditions is how aware the kids are of what they need in order to act as impelled readers, and how little of what they name is a method. I don't think reading teachers require new, more, or radical instructional techniques. The goal is straightforward. We need to figure out how our students can enjoy relationships with books and, as readers, with their teacher and one another.

My students like the solitude of the reading zone, and the quiet. They know how to be happily alone with a book. But they also recognize that the experiences of other readers help them keep themselves going. *This* is the rightful busywork of a reading class and a reading teacher. The ultimate delivery system for impelled reading is a deliberate environment that invites, nurtures, and sustains immersion in stories and characters, that says every day of every school year, *Welcome to the zone.*

CHAPTER 3

Choice

The grades 7–8 classroom library

aniel Pennac perfectly titled his paean to reading (1992). He called it *Better Than Life*. The frontispiece of the book is Pennac's list of what skilled, passionate, habitual, critical readers know but that teachers and parents can forget, don't understand, or do appreciate for themselves but withhold from children. My students and I read and debate it the first week of school; see his list at right.

Some of Pennac's ideas defend *how* a reader might read. His argument for reading out loud provokes the most discussion in my classroom, because so many student readers, those both struggling and strong, have a hard time performing aloud. To his "right not to finish," my kids have added a phrase: "or to read just the ending." And they proposed a number eleven: "The right to free access to lots of good books."

Others of Pennac's ideas address *what* someone might read. My kids voice the strong-

The Reader's Bill of Rights

1. The right not to read something

2. The right to skip pages

3. The right not to finish

4. The right to reread

5. The right to read anything

6. The right to escapism

7. The right to read anywhere

8. The right to browse

9. The right to read out loud

10. The right to not defend your tastes

—Daniel Pennac (1992)

est support for the right to one's own tastes as a reader. And they like Pennac's justification for free choice of books: "Our reasons for reading what we do are as eccentric as our reasons for living as we do."

In the classrooms at CTL, choice is a given: kids choose what they read because children who choose books are more likely to grow up to become adults who read books. Students who read only a steady diet of assigned titles don't get to answer, for themselves, the single most important question about book reading: why does anyone want to? As William Dean Howells put it, "The book which you read from a sense of duty, or because for any reason you must, does not commonly make friends with you."

I could no more pick *the* book that would invite a whole class to make friends with reading than I could decide who my students should grow up and marry. It's that personal, that chemical, that idiosyncratic, and, yes, to me anyway, that important. For students of every ability and background, it's the simple, miraculous act of reading a good book that turns them into readers, because even for the least experienced, most reluctant reader, it's the *one good book* that changes

A section of the kindergartners' classroom library

everything. The job of adults who care about reading is to move heaven and earth to put that book into a child's hands.

For me, the job begins on the first day of school, when I ask students to complete a survey (pages 29–30) about who they are as readers and what their good books might be. The questions are formatted over two pages, so there's plenty of room for students to respond.

Your Name _____

September Reading Survey

1. If you had to guess . . .

How many books would you say you owned? _____

How many books would you say there are in your house? _____

How many books would you say you've read since school let out in June? _____

How many books would you say you read during the last school year, September–June? _____

How many of *those* books did you choose for yourself? _____

2. What are the best three books you've ever read or had read aloud to you?

_____

_____

_____

3. In your ideal book, what would the main character be like?

_____

_____

_____

_____

_____

_____

4. What are your favorite genres, or kinds, of books?

_____

_____

5. Who are your favorite authors these days?

_____

_____

6. What are some of the ways you decide whether or not you'll read a book?

_____

_____

_____

_____

7. Have you ever liked a book so much that you reread it? _____ If so, can you name it/some of them here? _____

_____

8. What do you think someone has to know or do in order to be a strong, satisfied reader of books? _____

_____

_____

_____

_____

9. What do you think are your three greatest strengths as a reader of books?

_____

_____

_____

_____

10. What would you like to get better at? _____

_____

_____

_____

_____

11. Do you know the title of the next book you'd like to read? _____ If so, please tell me. _____

12. In general, how do you feel about reading and yourself as a reader?

_____

_____

_____

_____

I read the completed surveys and make a brief record—a one-page chart for the whole class, which I carry with me on my reading clipboard. On it I note students' recent histories as readers, number-of-books-wise and choosing-books-wise; the names of authors they like; the kind of main characters they want; if they've ever reread a beloved book, which is a good sign; if they have plans as readers, an even better sign; and how they perceive books and themselves as readers. And then I get to work, planning booktalks and trying to match the titles I know with the readers I'm getting to know.

My teaching work that is never done centers on the classroom library, that is, finding and replacing enough good books so there are titles for everyone and no reader gets left out. To reach that goal we need to have on hand *at least* 20 books per student.

A couple of times a month I visit a bookstore with a reliable collection of young adult literature, as well as inviting transitional titles—books by such writers as Isabel Allende, Margaret Atwood, Jonathan Safran Foer, Dave Eggers, Barbara Kingsolver, Yann Martel, Tim O'Brien, Richard Russo, and David Sedaris—that will give adolescents a taste of what comes next for them as independent readers. In the bookstore, I graze. I pick up every title that looks possible, bearing in mind authors and imprints that have been popular with my kids and thinking of individual students and what they love. Jonathan wants dystopian sci-fi; Nat: sports fiction; Nick: fantasy novels of the quest variety; Jed: Anne Rice; Tyler: edgy novels like *Catch-22, Rule of the Bone*, and *The Beach*; Noah: anything Irish; Brooks and Miles: strong plots and boy main characters who are easy to identify with.

I sit with the stack, skim first pages or chapters, and feel lucky when I find four or five titles I can imagine putting into a reader's hands or booktalking with genuine enthusiasm. Then, when I purchase them, I make sure I receive the teacher discount. Again, we're not investing in or replacing sixty-dollar anthologies, so the reading budget at CTL can be devoted to individual titles, mostly paperbacks, but some hardcovers when teachers can't wait.

I also read book reviews. I appreciate the way Teri Lesesne discusses young adult literature in *Voices from the Middle* and Don Gallo reviews it in *English Journal*. I read *Booklist*, which is published monthly, and the weekly *New York Times Book Review*. I talk to other seventh- and eighth-grade teachers about their finds.

And I've learned which awards and citations matter. On the back cover and inside the front cover of a paperback written for a young adult audience, I look for:

- ALA (American Library Association) Top Ten Best Books for Young Adults
- ALA Quick Pick for Reluctant Young Adult Readers
- ALA Alex Award Winner
- New York Public Library Books for the Teen Age
- National Book Award Winner or Finalist
- Coretta Scott King Award Winner
- Michael Printz Award for Excellence in Young Adult Literature
- *School Library Journal* Best Books of the Year
- *Kirkus Reviews* Editor's Choice
- Reference to a *starred* review in *Kirkus Reviews, Publishers Weekly, Booklist, The Horn Book,* or *School Library Journal*

I read a lot of young adult literature, and I do love it. But I do not and cannot read every book I add to the classroom library. First of all, I will never have that much time. I already suffer enough English-teacher guilt about the perfect, impossible job I should be doing. I read as many young adult titles as I can, and I read them as fast as I can. On a quiet weekend morning, I can skim at least one, sometimes two.

Secondly, I can no longer bring myself to read some of the books. These include science fiction, where Vonnegut is my limit; quest fantasies; techno-thrillers; or one more title by Dan Brown, Caroline B. Cooney, or Francesca Lia Block. But I have students who love—or would love—these genres and authors, and it's my responsibility to give them advice and direction.

So I've learned to pay attention to the experts in my classroom—to ask them to teach me about their genre specialties. When Jimmy was ready to go beyond Brian Jacques's Redwall series, I was ready with David Eddings, Philip Pullman, Robert Jordan, Jonathan Stroud, and Christopher Paolini, thanks to the fantasy-obsessed readers who preceded him. I'll also hand off a new book to a student I think might like it and ask if he or she would be willing to preview it and—if it's any good—booktalk it to the group.

I'm being realistic. I cannot read all the literature and also edit all the writing and plan all the lessons, write all the evaluations, attend all the meetings, and teach history, too. But I can become *intimate* enough with young adult literature to connect particular readers with the particular books they crave. *Intimacy* with my kids' books has become the goal.

I also developed an effective way for students to recommend good books to one another. Each grade level at our school has its own books-we-love case or stand. Students—not teachers—select the titles on display there. Sometimes a student booktalks the beloved title before adding it to the collection; sometimes a reader puts away a beloved book here, instead of reshelving it in the classroom library. And in June, all the boys and girls at our school help create master lists, organized by grade level and gender, of inviting, accessible titles.

Grades 5–6 readers and their library

The June lists contain the books our students name in response to this question: *What 10 to 12 books do you love so much that you think they might convince a ____-grade girl/boy who's a lot like you—except that she/he doesn't read much—that books are great?* The answers are available to our students and their parents over the summer, as well as other teachers and the general public, at our school's website, www.c-t-l.org, on the Kids Recommend page.

Students update the lists annually, because the field of children's literature changes so quickly. While a handful of titles do maintain their popularity over the years—S. E. Hinton's *The Outsiders* (1968), the novel that created the field of young adult literature, continues to speak to kids—most drop off and are replaced. I'll never again publish, between the covers of a book, a list of must-have titles for a classroom library. It will be out-of-date before the ink is dry.

Middle school teachers who download Kids Recommend will encounter book titles they'll recognize as having been challenged at other schools. In almost every case, the challenged book was assigned to a class by the teacher. In twenty years of teaching reading in a workshop in both private and public school classrooms, I can count on the fingers of one hand the times that parents raised concerns about a book that a student was reading. I think one reason I experience so few censorship problems is that I'm not passing out a class set of *The Catcher in the Rye* and requiring every student to read it. I am providing one copy in our classroom library for any student who's interested and ready. And in the end, as a parent, I bow to individual parents' wishes for their individual children.

Will's dad called me one evening in September because Will, a seventh grader from a devout family, had brought home an edgy teen novel that featured extreme swearing and some sexual activity. His father said he was offended by the language and thought Will was too young and inexperienced for the book's story and themes. I replied, "I absolutely respect your values, not to mention your sense of what's best for Will. Please tell him your objections to the book, and I'll help him look for another tomorrow during reading workshop. And thanks for calling me—I want you and Will's mom to be supportive of his reading and comfortable with his book choices. There are tons of other great titles I can put in his hands."

On a Monday morning of a different autumn, Zack's mother approached me in the school parking lot to complain that the Robert Cormier novel he read over the weekend had shaken him up. "He was upset all day yesterday," she said. "The harsh things that happened to the main character really troubled him. Zack can't handle books like this. He's more of a fantasy reader, I think." Again I said, "Thanks for telling me. You know, I'm just learning who Zack is, as a person and a reader. Some of the authors who write contemporary realism for young adults can be pretty bleak in their outlooks. I'll try to steer Zack away from this kind of book for now. I want his reading to satisfy him, not disturb him."

I'm a parent, too. The insights and concerns of my students' parents matter to me. So when a mother or father speaks to me about a child's book choice, I respond in the context of the particular child. Censorship hasn't been an issue at CTL or in my previous public school experience. I think this is the case because each child chooses his or her books, because I'm not deciding what anyone *has* to read, and because I've read many of the books. I know what's in them. In the end, if put to the test, I recognize when I can defend a title's inclusion in our classroom library, and when I cannot.

This means that in addition to purchasing books, I return them. When I read a young adult novel or a series and can find nothing of value, literary or otherwise, I ask for the school's money back. I try hard not to buy junk—there is more than enough of it available to my students in pop culture, always. I don't purchase many adult best sellers, either, and I talk with students about the differences between popular page-turners and literary novels. On occasion I borrow a best seller from the local library or download a chapter from the Internet, read a bit aloud, and ask kids what they notice. For students who have been reading literary, young adult fiction, James Patterson and Nora Roberts are a shock: "How can this be a best seller? Who could read that and think it's good writing?"

But at the same time that my students recognize that Dan Brown and Michael Crichton don't write lucid prose or develop believable characters they can care about, they also say, "The bad writing bothered me, but not as much as the plot grabbed me. I was turning the pages like crazy just to see what would happen." There are insights to be gained even from a page-turner—I think understanding the definition is a huge one. The insights come in the context of continuous conversations about what makes a book worth a reader's precious time.

There are too many good books out there, waiting for us, for a reader to spend precious time with a book he or she isn't enjoying. Students need more than permission to abandon books that aren't satisfying them. They need encouragement from a teacher, and even the occasional cease and desist order.

A kid who hasn't found that one good book yet will sit for weeks with a title that bores him because he doesn't know how the reading zone feels. Teachers need to be confident enough to take books *out* of readers' hands when they're not loving them, then give the child three or four great books as new possibilities. And we need to help kids think and talk about their criteria for book abandonment: how many pages will you give a book to become compelling before you pull the plug? The most important "should" in reading workshop is always the same: students should read for the joy of reading. Once they have the reading habit, the books themselves will form their tastes.

Children's author Philip Pullman wrote, "True education flowers at the point when delight falls in love with responsibility. If you love something, you want to look after it" (2005). One way we show children that we love them is by looking after them as readers. Only when we invite them to find books that delight them is it likely that they will come to cherish literature and their own literacy.

CHAPTER 4

Ease

The seventh and eighth graders' display of books they love

In our faculty handbook at CTL, the section on reading begins with a quotation from Frank Smith: "Children learn to read only by reading. Therefore, the only way to facilitate their learning to read is to make reading easy for them" (1983).

I put it there to brush away, right from the start, the cobwebs—and outright spiderwebs—of the long history of frustrating, cumbersome, "teacher-proof" systems of reading instruction. Smith reminds me and my colleagues that when it comes to reading, our job is to understand it, notice what needs to be taught, teach it, and, in all ways, *ease the way* for students to become skilled, passionate, habitual, critical readers.

This is pretty much the opposite of what I was taught in undergraduate methods courses, where I learned how to teach assigned novels one at a time, a chapter at a time, with discussions, tests, and even essays at the ends of chapters. The emphasis was dual: Make it hard—*rigorous* was the preferred term. And make students prove they read the books and got what they were supposed to get. It was the same method that had been inflicted on me in middle and high school and that ruined certain books for me for years—*The Light in the Forest*, *My Ántonia*, *The Great Gatsby*, *Moby-Dick*, *The Scarlet Letter*, *Pride and Prejudice*. My experience as a student of reading taught me that there was a right book to read and a right way to read it, and it was supposed to hurt.

Learning to read and read well is already hard enough: it takes years of practice to make knowledge of reading automatic, transparent, and fluid. When children practice reading in a context that's kind—with books they love, teachers who understand reading, and systems devised to make a hard thing easier—they're more inclined to practice, remember, make sense of, get better at, and love reading.

To make reading easy for students, the bottom-line requirement is an inviting classroom library, organized so it's simple for children to find good books and return them. The Dewey decimal system doesn't have a place here. Instead, teachers need to put books together in ways that help young readers find what they're looking for, even if they don't yet know what it is.

Twenty-five years ago, when I began to learn about young adult literature, my classroom library arrangement was crude: fiction, nonfiction, and poetry. Today, I shelve over 1,200 books, alphabetically by authors' last names, in bookcases labeled in useful, inviting categories: memoirs and journalism, humor, fantasy, science fiction, thrillers, horror and supernatural, sports fiction, historical fiction, war and antiwar, free-verse novels and memoirs, graphic novels and histories, poetry anthologies, poetry collections, short story collections, classics, drama, essay collections, and—the largest grouping—contemporary realistic fiction.

In addition, I set out new titles and featured authors separately, and my students maintain their books-we-love collection. We display these books at the front of the classroom with their covers facing out, so they're even more inviting and accessible.

Books I don't—won't—stock anywhere in the classroom library include *The Guinness Book of World Records*, collections of sports statistics, comic books, repair manuals for dirt bikes, guides to computer gaming, Chicken Soup anthologies, and teen celebrity bios. If my goal is for students to get lost in the zone, the volumes I put into their hands must, through the power of strong narrative threads, be compelling enough to pull every kind of kid into the realm of stories.

Over the years I've lost a lot of books from the classroom library, or rather, my students have "lost" a lot of my books. While one part of me delighted that students were loving books so much that they were borrowing them forever, another part fumed at the cost—both the price I paid to purchase a book and the lack of availability to other readers of a beloved title. I went back and forth between elaborate check-out systems, which ate up my time, and freedom from systems, which ate up my books.

What works, finally, is the simplest approach of all. Teachers of grades 1–8 write the name of each student in our classes on a few 4-by-6-inch index cards. We staple each child's cards together, then file them in an unlidded box, one box per class, along with a pencil or two. When a reader borrows a book, he finds his set of book cards in his class's box and writes the new title. When a reader returns a book, she brings her card set *and* the book—the ocular proof, as we say—to the teacher, who draws a line through the title and writes his or her initials next to it. Then the reader shelves the book. Most often I initial titles back into the classroom library as I circulate among students during reading workshop. Today, instead of a third or more of the volumes in the classroom library disappearing, only a handful go missing each year.

To make book borrowing, reading at home, and returning easy for our youngest readers, CTL provides the means of conveyance. The school hires a parent with a sewing machine to construct overnight bookbags for students in grades K–4. We use bright, sturdy, fabric remnants to create 16-by-12½-by-3-inch bags, with double handles made from 1-by-26-inch straps of webbing. This gift from the school is a child's to keep for the year and another demonstration of how much the teachers value books and reading. The teachers help each K–4 student make sure there's a book in the bag at the end of reading workshop to go home

Above: One class's set of book-borrowing cards

Right: On the reader's card, initialing a book's return to the classroom library

that afternoon and return via the bookbag in the morning. In June, we collect the overnight bookbags; wash, repair, and replace them as necessary; then put them back to work in September.

Older students wouldn't be caught dead with bright, sturdy, fabric bookbags. Kids in grades 5–8 carry their books back and forth between school and home in backpacks. But their teachers, too, make sure that every student *has* a book to pack up every day at the end of reading workshop.

And to make home reading easier for all our students, we do not assign busywork in connection with the pleasures of books. There are no home-reading slips, book reports, sticky notes, double-entry journals, or other documentation that serves to check up on, test, eat the time of, and kill the joy of readers. We trust that the books are great. We trust that the kids will love them. We understand that any reader who gets lost in the zone dreads the prospect of busywork when he or she closes a book. We acknowledge that it *serves no purpose*. Because we talk with our students about their reading, in the conversations of reading workshop, teachers can easily ascertain whether everyone is loving and understanding his or her book.

The approach we use to determine whether students are understanding their books—that is, whether a title is a good match with a child's abilities as a reader—was developed by Leslie Funkhauser, a second-grade teacher in New Hampshire (Hansen, 1987). When children choose what they will read, they must be able to differentiate between books that are within their reach and books that aren't—yet. So we define three levels of book difficulty, teach kids the definitions, and use the language in our conversations about reading.

For every student, a given title is either a Holiday or easy read; a Challenge, which will require some adult assistance; or a Just Right, that is, a book that's appropriate in terms of the child's current needs and level of skill. One easy test for a Just Right is Jeanette Veatch's "rule of thumb" (1968). A reader turns to a page in the middle of the book that he or she is considering, reads it silently, and puts down a finger at each unfamiliar word. If the child hits five words—uses up all four fingers and a thumb—that's an indication that a title is too difficult: for now, it's still a Challenge book for this reader. In a fall newsletter to parents about reading (included in Chapter 10), we teach parents in depth about Holidays, Just Rights, and Challenges, so they can continue to help children at home do what they're trying to do as readers.

CTL teachers appreciate this system because it's easy—a few simple-to-determine levels—and because it labels the books, not the children. All of us, as readers, have our own Holidays, Just Rights, and Challenges. The three kinds of books help students consider where they stand in relation to a particular title at a particular moment in their reading lives, without undermining their confidence by labeling them, and without narrowing their reading experience to selections predetermined to be written at the right "level."

And the reading teachers of CTL *teach reading*. We tell our students what we know, what we notice *they* know and don't know yet, and how they can better do and understand what they're trying to do and understand. In lessons to the whole group, taught before individuals settle into independent reading time, we provide information, conduct demonstrations, and lead discussions that help children make sense of all kinds of reading and all kinds of books.

At the primary level, this means that Helene Coffin, at kindergarten, and Ted DeMille, at grades 1–2, teach their students lessons about the strategies that beginning readers use to identify unfamiliar words in the books they're reading. They show the children how to look at the beginning letters of the word; use what they've learned about letter sounds, from their own writing during writing workshop, and see if sounding out will work here; look at an illustration for clues; listen for a repeating pattern; listen for a rhyming pattern; look for a little word they do know inside the bigger word they don't; skip the unfamiliar word, read the rest of the sentence, and then come back and try it again; use a placeholder word and just keep going; try to recall whether they've seen the word before somewhere else; and ask for help.

Helene and Ted also teach procedural lessons about what reading workshop should look, sound, and feel like. They introduce high-frequency words. They teach children how to read one another's names. They discuss with their classes when it pays to reread and when it's better to keep going; how readers pause, breathe, and assimilate at a period; why and how to keep track of finished books one has read; how to take a bookwalk through a picture book; how to preview front- and back-cover blurbs and chapter titles to determine where a chapter book is headed; how to mine the table of contents, index, glossary, and diagrams in non-fiction texts; and the elements of stories—plot, character, setting, problem, climax, and resolution. They also engage their kids in studies, via read-alouds and discussions, of authors and illustrators whose books offer generous invitations to young readers: Jan Brett, Eric Carle, Donald Crew, Tomie dePaola, Lois Ehlert, Mem Fox, Gail Gibbons, Kevin Henkes, Shirley Hughes, Leo Lionni, Arnold Lobel, Bill Martin, Jr., Robert McCloskey, Else Holmelund Minarik, Jerry Pallotta, Patricia Polacco, Maurice Sendak, William Steig. The primary-grade teachers read aloud hundreds of fiction and nonfiction storybooks every year, and they help their students read, recite, and sing hundreds of poems, songs, chants, and daily messages printed on chart paper or projected on overhead transparencies.

This isn't everything Helene Coffin and Ted DeMille do as reading teachers—they have their own books to write and stories to tell. What I want to suggest here are the nature and range of lessons that make reading *easier* for beginners: instruction that brings knowledge, joy, purpose, skill, personal preference, and a sense of community to reading instruction at the primary level. This represents a parallel universe to the nonsense lessons that dominate textbook publishers' programs for beginning readers—the kits and basals that confuse looking busy with reading and that deny young children the pleasures of the zone.

At the other end of the K–8 spectrum, I teach lessons to my middle-school classes that make it easier for individuals both to enter the zone and to get their feet under them as opinionated, versatile, critical readers who have goals and plans. Many of the lessons are booktalks. Each involves kids in a discussion of good books and good things that smart readers know.

In the fall I teach about reading as a psycholinguistic process; that is, I illustrate how the eye and brain process text and demonstrate why the path to fluent reading is regular, voluminous, silent reading (Smith, 1997; Weaver, 1994). I review the expectations and rules for reading workshop. We talk about how and why to develop criteria for choosing books and abandoning them; the usefulness of keeping a personal reading record and a list of "someday" books; and how the act of looking for and naming favorites—books, authors, genres, poems, poets—eases the way to becoming both a happy, literate reader *and* one who can take control of his or her literary life.

My kids and I discuss where to find great reads beyond the classroom library. I teach them about the different stances readers take in relation to different kinds of texts—the *aesthetic* mode, a.k.a. the zone, when we're reading for the pleasure of the "lived-through experience," and the *efferent* mode, in which we read in order to acquire information—and how one's frame of mind shifts one's approach to a text (Rosenblatt, 1980; 1983). We consider criteria for pace—when do readers decide to speed up, slow down, skip, skim, or look ahead? We talk about why and when readers want to reread books and poems, and we name the genres we're reading—the most recent genre summary we collaborated on appears in Chapter 10.

I also teach about the books, styles, experiences, and perspectives of authors and poets who write well for middle school readers. I show kids how poetry works, in terms of its forms, sound patterns, diction, compression, and use of figurative language, and how to read a poem (Atwell, 2006). I illustrate the elements of literary fiction—character development, problem, plot, pace, plausibility, narrative voice, lead and conclusion, climax, tone, theme, and resolution. I account for the differences among a vignette, short story, novella, and novel. I describe the structure of a short story; how effective essays, memoirs, and parodies work; what a sequel, a trilogy, and a series are; and what various awards and citations mean. I relate relevant trivia about how book publishing works—royalties, printings, copyright dates, jacket blurbs, and the hardbound-to-paperback route. And I introduce resources from the worlds of publishing and scholarship that are worthwhile for middle school readers to know about, from *Booklist*, to *The New York Times Book Review*, to Amazon.com and Salon.com reviews, to *Masterpieces of World Literature in Digest Form* (Magill, 1991) and *Benét's Reader's Encyclopedia* (Murphy, 1996).

A teacher's goal at CTL, as a planner of lessons, is to provide information that's useful to readers. In combination with useful time—all the hours at school and home devoted to reading stories and visiting the zone—most of our students ease their way into becoming skilled, passionate, habitual, critical readers. But even with smart, sensible teaching, some children will struggle. We give these students slightly different vehicles for entering the reading zone.

Some of our struggling readers lack experience with books. They come to CTL with normal intelligence, a lot of background in nonsense instruction, and little to none as choosers, readers, and lovers of books. Standardized reading tests have placed them anywhere between one and three years below grade level.

More than anything else that a school can provide them, these struggling readers need surefire stories written near—or not impossibly above—their independent reading levels, and time to read them. They need *pleasure*. Their teachers need to dedicate ourselves to not resting until we've found the first book that can deliver it; most often, it's a novel with an extreme plot and stronger-than-usual characters. Only frequent, sustained, voluminous reading will bring these readers up to grade level. Every September I recognize the challenge and, ultimately, satisfaction of nudging one or more inexperienced readers into the zone, through main characters and stories that compel them to believe in books, to practice reading, and to perceive themselves as the kind of people who read and who like it.

Some of my struggling readers are boys and girls who struggle in general—their intelligence tests below average norms, with no evidence of learning disabilities. These kids, too, want to be able to read at the top of their ability range *and* to enter the zone as easily and joyfully as their classmates do. So I add to the classroom library, booktalk, and recommend titles for readers who aren't able to interpret subtleties of motivation or theme, who can't appreciate ambiguity or irony, who don't revel in metaphor or beautiful diction, but who still want and deserve the zone.

For these two groups of readers—the inexperienced and the challenged—imprints such as Orca Soundings and authors such as Amelia Atwater-Rhodes, Francesca Lia Block, Meg Cabot, Caroline B. Cooney, Robert Cormier, Mel Glenn, Homer Hickam, Jr., S. E. Hinton, Anthony Horowitz, Gordon Korman, Walter Dean Myers, Gary Paulsen, Louis Sachar, Sonya Sones, and Wendelien Van Draanen have succeeded in creating strong characters and plots that can transport them into the reading zone.

Other struggling readers cope with identified learning disabilities, which interfere with their ability to process text. In other words, their intelligence ranges from average to far above, but their performance as readers, affected by dyslexia or other processing difficulties, does not. Because of neurological differences, they cannot access all the cuing systems that other readers rely on. But they can develop and retain sight vocabularies that, eventually, allow them to read with fluency, understanding, and pleasure. Here, a key is linking auditory and visual input, especially during the critical primary and intermediate-grade years.

At CTL, when we were first starting out, this meant lining up aides, volunteers, parents, or older students who were fluent oral readers to sit side by side with a student every day and read aloud a book the child chose, as he or she followed along and matched the reader's voice with the words on the page. Then we began to purchase audiotapes of the picture books that children loved. We created a books-on-cassette center, with a half dozen tape recorders, sets of headphones, and a small library of books and tapes organized in plastic bags. This gave learning-disabled children greater independence, but the school could never afford enough book-and-tape sets, and, more significantly, the taped books were performed rather than read. The interpretations were charming, but the voices were too fast and idiosyncratic for beginning readers to reliably match voice and print.

Next, a parent of a young student diagnosed with dyslexia contacted the National Library Service (NLS) for the Blind and Physically Handicapped. Through their talking books program, NLS loans thousands of audiobooks on tape cassettes or CDs that are recorded to play at slower-than-standard speed. They also provide headphones and specially adapted CD players or tape recorders—what we call "reading machines." All of this is available at no cost, sent and returned by postage-free mail, through a network of cooperating regional libraries.

Talking books are a godsend for learning-disabled students who qualify for the program. Jill Cotta, who teaches our third and fourth graders, believes that the speed control on the reading machine is key: kids slow down the reading rate of each selection until they can follow the words with their eyes. She also notes that the adult voices on the NLS audiobooks read at one pace, with little inflection, interpretation, or variation in volume, and without special accents or pitches customized for different characters. Finally, there are no sound effects or background music to distract readers from the sound and sight of one word after another in the books they've chosen. Talking books help young students connect auditory and visual input, enter the zone, and, over time, develop sight vocabularies that compensate for reading disabilities.

To be eligible for the program, a sighted child must be certified by his or her physician as having a physically or visually based disability severe enough that it makes it difficult to read books. Students with nonorganic reading problems—for example, short attention spans, emotional issues, deprived backgrounds, different first languages—don't qualify. A disabled child's parents apply for talking books on his or her behalf, their physician signs the application form, and, if approved, only that student may use the audiobooks and reading machine. If a child is a legitimate candidate for talking books, the process is simple and quick.

The NLS publishes online catalogues of available audiobooks on their Web site at http://www.loc.gov/nls/. The collection does not include recorded textbooks or other curriculum materials, just lots of good fiction and nonfiction titles. Jill helps her learning-disabled students choose titles from the classroom library that they wish to read; then she or a parent orders the accompanying audiobooks, usually three at a time. Most often, the talking books arrive in the next day's mail.

Once our LD students hit fifth or sixth grade, the "big, clunky machine"—as their next teacher, Glenn Powers, puts it—can become a drawback. Self-conscious eleven-year-olds fare better with a small tape recorder, headphones, and, by then, the pace and inflection of regular books on tape, which Glenn borrows through the public interlibrary-loan system.

The process of choosing titles—and helping children choose well—is the same for Jill's and Glenn's learning-disabled readers as it is for everyone else in their classes. These readers, too, listen to booktalks and friends' and the teacher's recommendations and decide what sounds good, before their teacher orders it on tape. They, too, confer with Jill and Glenn about their choices: Even with a tape, is this book a Just Right for you? Can you follow its plot and themes? Will it help you develop your knowledge of print and your sight vocabulary? And, sometimes: Does its attraction lie more in its potential as great entertainment to listen to, rather than a text you can read along with and practice on?

A crucial difference that Jill and Glenn do observe in disabled student readers is a tendency to choose books that are too hard. These kids know they're not yet reading as their peers are. Sometimes they try to compensate, or to impress other readers in their class, by selecting titles that are Challenges-plus. Glenn and Jill have learned to level with L.D. students about what they need to be practicing as readers, and at the same time help them discover and articulate their tastes and preferences as lovers of books.

At CTL we haven't made a single scientific breakthrough in reading instruction. Instead, we try to notice what individual children can and can't do in the context of reading books. Then we look for ways to ease the process. And we make sure that our students who need the *most* sense and satisfaction—those who struggle as readers—get it.

I remember the final pupil evaluation team (PET) meeting I attended on behalf of Samuel, a CTL student diagnosed with dyslexia. It was June, and the point of this PET was whether Sam should continue to be classified as special ed next year, as a high school freshman. His parents and I argued it wasn't necessary: in seventh and eighth grades, Sam had read thirty-eight titles on his own. All the time he'd spent reading books along with someone else's voice as a young student, and then venturing into the zone independently in middle school via characters and stories he loved, had given him a sight vocabulary that would choke a horse.

But the special-ed tester from the school district Samuel's family lived in argued that he was still severely disabled. As evidence, she showed us the dreadful results of his most recent screening: he still couldn't sound out a long list of made-up morphemes.

If this is how someone chooses to define reading—as the pronunciation of nonsense syllables in isolation—Samuel will never be a reader. But bring on great *books*, and he can read virtually any title he picks up. His rich, frequent, sustained experiences with the built-in redundancies of English syntax and semantics, his acquired memory of the sizes and shapes of thousands of words, and his interest in stories enabled Sam—over time and with much joyful practice—to vault over his dyslexia and become a reader. He did enter high school as a regular student. So far, he has achieved the honor roll every trimester.

There's yet another group of struggling readers—one with whom I don't have experience, because of our location in rural Maine. So far, few new immigrants have settled here; there are only a handful among our parent population, and all of their children were born in the U.S. But nationwide these days, one out of every five children is either an immigrant or has parents who are (Suárez-Orozco & Suárez-Orozco, 2001). The most practical and convincing research into the reading development of minority-language children, as reported by Stephen Krashen and others (2006), demonstrates two crucial phenomena.

First, learning to read in one's native language makes it easier to become a reader of English. As Krashen puts it, it takes considerably less effort on anyone's part "to understand text in a language you already know." He makes another essential point: "And once you can read, you can read. Reading ability transfers across languages." In spite of a backlash in many places against bilingual education, when it comes to teaching reading, it only makes sense to do the easy thing: invite children to develop as readers in their first language, then help them put their knowledge and experience of print to work in their new language.

In addition, Krashen's summary of the research shows that once students have learned to read in their first language and are beginning to speak English, a reading workshop approach is ideal: free reading of texts written in English provides "a clear route to English literacy and the development of academic English." In other words, the same access to good books and time to read them are key for language-minority children, too, to become skilled, passionate, habitual, critical readers—not to mention informed citizens of their new country and full participants in the community of readers of books, with all the knowledge, understanding, and power to be found there.

James Baldwin wrote about books, "You think your pain and your heartbreak are unprecedented in the history of the world, but then you read. It was books that taught me that the things that tormented me most were the very things that connected me with all the people who were alive, or who had ever been alive." Only a teacher who opens wide the door to the reading zone can ensure that *all* students experience the mutuality of the human race. Only in books will children experience the people, ideas, events, and feelings that make existence comprehensible. Strong readers *and* struggling readers want to know the joys and sorrows of other lives, the common dreams that unite us, and the satisfactions of great stories. Teachers help by making reading *as easy as possible* for all of our students all of the time.

I think teachers know this. But we get sidetracked by trends in methods, or misled into believing that, somehow, there's a more direct or effective test prep than time with books—or we're outright ordered to use programs that waste our students' time and kill their interest in reading.

This is why tenure was invented. Contrary to certain propaganda, tenure exists not to protect the job security of bad teachers but to safeguard smart teachers' decisions about what matters and how best to help children learn it. A tenured reading teacher in a district that mandates nonsense can call it that. He or she can also shortcut the program wherever and however possible, close the classroom door, invite frequent, voluminous, happy encounters with books, and create a haven for readers that will change those kids for a lifetime.

The good teachers I know of every grade and subject are in the classroom because they want to influence kids for a lifetime, to make a difference over the long haul, to inspire students to become thoughtful, productive grown-ups. No one grows up and celebrates the teachers who assigned all the readings, corrected all the worksheets, counted all the sticky notes, and followed the prescribed curriculum.

Instead, we remember the teachers whose clubs we wanted to join (Smith, 1988). Their invitations were generous and joyful, and they cleared the way for us to do work that mattered for the rest of our lives. The reading teachers we recall with gratitude weren't Holidays; nor were they Challenges. As kindergarten poet Ryland has already learned, influential teachers of reading make a hard thing feel easy and worthwhile: they are *just right*.

Ryland, in the reading zone

Helene's My Just Right

by Ryland

I love the way Helene helps me.

I feel cozy when she hugs me.

When Helene hugs me

I'm in a cozy room

all by myself with pillows all around me.

If Helene didn't help me

I wouldn't be able to read just rights.

All the books would tumble off the shelves

and I wouldn't know which were just right for me.

And I'd spend all my time picking up all the books.

And soon it would be snack.

And reading would be over.

And I wouldn't have a just right in my hand.

I love the way Helene helps me.

Helene is my just right.

CHAPTER 5

Comprehension

A seventh grader lives among characters in a young adult novel

I've represented myself in these pages as a teacher who tries to understand and teach reading, rather than orchestrate methods and activities. But I need to tell a story on myself, one with at least two morals. The first is how easy it is to be seduced by new methods, especially when they arrive wrapped in research. The second underlines how important it is for teachers to be able to think straight about reading comprehension—to make distinctions between study skills that *do* help readers gain concepts and information in science and history, and metacognitive strategies that *may* interrupt children's processing of stories and distract them from the pleasures of the reading zone. But first, the story.

In the 1990s, I jumped—*vaulted* is a more accurate verb—onto the comprehension-strategy bandwagon, when educational researchers (Pearson, 1985; Pearson, Roehler, Dole, & Duffy, 1992) identified the seven comprehension strategies—that is, the seven cognitive processes—used by proficient readers whenever we read:

- activating prior knowledge—and creating visual, auditory, and tactile associations (a.k.a. *schemas*)—before, during, and after reading

- determining the most important ideas and themes in a text

- asking questions

- drawing inferences and conclusions

- monitoring understanding

- retelling and synthesizing

- utilizing fix-up strategies to repair comprehension when it breaks down

Educators who designed methods rooted in this work determined that if students were explicitly taught the seven strategies, then directed to practice them whenever they read, they'd become better comprehenders of texts and more successful readers.

I was intrigued. Frankly, I was also a little relieved. Despite everything I recognized and celebrated about the impact of frequent, voluminous, enjoyable experiences with books on my students' abilities as readers, I still harbored a pocket of doubt about the rigor of reading workshop, especially about my role in it. I'd long since rejected the model of an English teacher as someone who assigns novels a chapter at a time, tests kids on themes and details, and collects book reports. But I hadn't yet defined, to my own satisfaction, exactly what I was supposed do as the teacher in a reading workshop. So the comprehension strategies held immediate

A kindergartner in the zone

appeal: I could give myself a role by teaching these.

Here was a new kind of rigor, a metacognitive version with a basis in science. While it's true that I hadn't actually read any of the research reports, I inhaled the articles and books that described the methods based on them. It wasn't until later that I discovered that the evidence for teaching the comprehension strategies consisted of short-term studies, some of questionable design, of several handfuls of students. What the results seemed to show, at best, was that given instruction in and practice with study skills, and given more time to read the passages on tests, some kids scored slightly higher on some tests of reading comprehension. Researcher Ronald Carver, in an exhaustive analysis of the cited studies, found serious problems with their designs, questioned the researchers' interpretations of the data, and reached a similar conclusion:

> After reviewing all of this recent evidence that purportedly supports the teaching of comprehension skills or strategies, it appears reasonable to summarize these data with two separate statements. First, when students are given material that they cannot comprehend well when they read it as they normally do, they can be taught certain study skills that will increase their accuracy of comprehension. Second, when students are given a specific reading task, such as answering main idea questions, they can be instructed or trained to answer these questions better with guided practice, but there is no evidence that this skill will transfer to more global reading comprehension skills. Therefore, if educators are most concerned with helping students become better comprehenders in general, as is commonly measured by standardized tests of reading comprehension or

informal reading inventories, there is no evidence that the currently touted instructional practices are beneficial (1987, p. 124).

But for me, that recognition was still a long way off. Now, fueled by reading about methods based on the research, I was ready to teach the seven strategies of proficient readers—eager to reenter my reading workshop armed with a new curriculum of demonstrations and activities, most of them centered on reading schemas, that is, asking students to consider what they already know in relation to a reading selection and to generate explicit associations or "connections." The three major linkages were described as text-to-oneself, text-to-another-text, and text-to-larger-world connections.

In practice, this means that teachers model the schemas for students: we select a story for reading aloud, plan and rehearse the connections we'll make, then read the text to students and interrupt ourselves to describe our text-to-self, text-to-text, and text-to-world connections. Students are directed to do the same—to stop during independent reading, brainstorm for similar kinds of connections, and, when they make one, articulate it, most often by writing it down on a sticky note and attaching it to the page where the connection was achieved. Students can also create bulletin board displays that chronicle the connections they made as they read a story, and Venn diagrams to show relationships among strategies. Or they might focus on one strategy—say, asking questions—and practice it every time they read. Or they're instructed to pause during their reading of a story to visualize and sketch an image inspired by the writing. Readers who struggle with a particular strategy can be assigned to a strategy study group until they're able to make connections, form visual images, draw inferences, and so on.

In I plunged. I explained proficient reader research and schema theory to my students. I prepared, rehearsed, and modeled a connection-packed read-aloud of a short story by Robert Cormier. Then I passed out individual pads of self-sticking notes and invited kids to activate their existing schema, connect these to the new schema that emerged as they read, and capture it all on the sticky notes.

My students were kind. They indulged me for about three weeks. Then came the rebellion. Readers asked for a class meeting, and they let loose on the comprehension strategies.

Metacognition was interfering with the reading zone. The sticky notes intruded in the zone, disrupted the flow of a great story, ate up precious hours that could have been devoted to living inside another great story, and wasted their time as readers. Not one student could name a positive effect of the strategies on his or her reading performance. Asa pointed out that in a book like *In Cold Blood*, he didn't *want* to make any connections with any of the characters, plus he was trying hard to avoid visuals. Tom said he had gone back into one of his beloved David Eddings fantasy novels after he finished it, invented just enough connections to make me happy, then sprinkled them among the pages of the novel. "I want to live with Garian and experience his adventures when I'm reading my book," he said, "and you want me to stop and take notes." And Rachel observed that someone could do all seven things on the list of behaviors of proficient readers and still be uncertain about the meaning of what she had just read.

Uh-oh.

Even worse, I realized later, a reader could activate all seven strategies, hate what a book was about, find serious fault with its author, have a perfectly miserable time reading it, and learn that the point of reading stories was to swallow your opinions and articulate your connections. And, worst of all, a reader could become as proficient as hell according to the list but *never ever enter the reading zone*—never become immersed in a great story, experience the life of a character, escape from his or her own life, dream, laugh, despair, celebrate, understand, wonder, or fall in love.

I apologized to my students and collected the pads of sticky notes. I invited them back into the zone, via a workshop once again free of busywork and rich with lessons about reading and literature. And I began to try to make sense of what had happened.

My questions sent me back to the work of literary theorist Louise Rosenblatt. In *Literature as Exploration* (1938; 1983), her classic book about reader response, and in my favorite of her essays, "What Facts Does This Poem Teach You?" (1980), Rosenblatt defines two modes of reading: *efferent* and *aesthetic*. She observes that these are parallel frames of mind, existing on a continuum, which any reader brings to bear during every act of reading in order to create meaning.

When we approach a text in an efferent frame of mind—from the Latin *effere*, which means "to carry away"—we're reading in order to acquire information. We focus our attention on what we'll learn. Recent examples from my own reading experience that I'd describe as mainly efferent include Sara Mead's report "The Truth About Boys and Girls" (2006), the front section of yesterday's *New York Times*, the directions for a pressure washer I rented from our local hardware store, and a third, skimming reread of Frank Smith's *Essays into Literacy* (1983). In each instance, I was focused primarily on facts and ideas I could learn and carry away, perhaps to act on in some way, but not necessarily.

A young reader "lives through" a story

The aesthetic stance parallels that of efferent reading; when a reader assumes it, he or she fuses affective and cognitive elements together into what Rosenblatt calls "a personally lived-through poem or story." We read aesthetically for its own sake, for the pleasures and rewards of living vicariously inside someone else's literary world. I think the aesthetic mode has a lot in common with the state that my students, as readers of stories, have named the reading zone.

In considering the reading of schoolchildren, Rosenblatt noted the difficulties that arise when teachers direct students to read from an efferent stance texts that kids are inclined to approach aesthetically—that is, to find and carry away information *from a story*. She was concerned that twentieth-century teachers were asking students not to "live through" and love literature but to find facts: main ideas, supporting details, causes and effects, plot events, settings, character motivations. In the 1980s, the theories of Louise Rosenblatt showed me how I did—and didn't—want to ask my students to respond to their reading.

Rosenblatt's work is as relevant today, in the realm of twenty-first century reading instruction. It seems to me that a comprehension-strategy approach asks students to take an efferent stance every time they read, regardless of the text or their purpose in reading it; that is, it teaches children that when they read stories, rather than living through them and experiencing "the attractions of the journey itself" (Rosenblatt, 1978), they're supposed to seek and carry away information. In this case, the information takes the form of strategy data. Now, it's connections, questions, conclusions, and visual images—instead of main ideas and supporting details—that threaten to undermine a young reader's experience of a story. And when it comes to the reading zone, and a child's ability to enter and enjoy it, I think that directing story readers to activate comprehension strategies may *hurt* their comprehension.

Let me illustrate what I mean with an example from my own experience. I had picked up *Silent to the Bone* (2000), a young adult novel by E. L. Konigsburg, and I was in the zone, thinking and feeling along with Connor, the narrator. He mentions that a comatose baby, the mystery of whose abuse lies at the heart of the novel, was born on the fourth of July. And without wanting or meaning to, I drifted off into a little reverie about Jimmy, a seventh-grade student who made it a game to tell me wild lies with the poker face of all time, just to see if he could deceive me. Once, when he claimed he was born on the fourth of July, I bet him a dollar he wasn't. Then I looked up his birth date in the school records and had to fork over the cash.

At almost the same moment, a strain of the George M. Cohan song "The Yankee Doodle Boy" and an image of Jimmy Cagney tap dancing floated through my brain. And then I remembered that friends and rivals Thomas Jefferson and John Adams died on the same fourth of July, Jefferson first, although Adams didn't know it—his last words were "Thomas Jefferson still lives."

Finally I shook my head to clear it of these idiosyncratic connections—every one of them a distraction from living through a great story—and dived back into Konigsburg's words and the feelings they called forth in me about the character Branwell's confusion and anguish—about the power of shame as an emotion.

Someone versed in comprehension-strategy pedagogy will recognize that in a few seconds with *Silent to the Bone*, and entirely in spite of myself, I activated all three schemas. I made text-to-self, text-to-text, and text-to-world connections that had nothing to do with my feeling-thinking experience of Konigsburg's writing. These connections were unwelcome by-products of a waking brain, not indications of my comprehension of the novel.

Worse, the connections bumped me out of the reading zone. They removed me from my meaningful experience of the lives of the characters and the beauty and power of Konigsburg's language. Although I'll tolerate random connections when I'm in the grip of an aesthetic experience—so do we all—I don't seek them out. They're just something the human brain seems wired to do. When it's the reading zone I'm after, text-to-self, text-to-text, and text-to-world connections aren't necessarily signs that I'm comprehending. They can also represent brief obstacles to my immersion in a fictional world.

In fact, a more useful lesson about the connections that story readers make, as we're reading, is one that helps students decide *how to respond to them*. I ask my kids, "When you're reading a story, do you ever bump yourself out of the zone because something in the book sparks a thought or a memory?" and follow up with, "If so, how do you respond to the bump?"

My students determined that there are *relevant* and *irrelevant bumps*. And this turns out to be a useful distinction, versus categorizing associations as text-to-self, text-to-text, and text-to-world, because it gives readers of stories some control over how they'll respond to distractions.

A relevant distraction—or bump—includes the moments when we stop living inside a story because we've noticed something about how it is written—how beautifully the author has phrased something or how terribly, how long the paragraphs are, how the dialogue has been set off, how a word is spelled, or, in the case of a typo, misspelled. Frank Smith calls these the occasions when we *read like writers* (1988): we pay attention to the way a text is written, and we enjoy an efferent moment as we observe something in someone else's writing that we might choose to carry away, and put to use, in writing of our own.

My kids also nominated, as relevant bumps, instances when they stop and consider what a word means or how it might be pronounced, figure out a mys-

An eighth grader in the zone comprehends a memoir

tery, understand suddenly where the plot is headed, realize they're confused about what's happening, wonder if there's a sequel or when the book was written, or recall a similar character or plot development from another story.

We determined that a relevant bump deserves at least a moment of respect—a *hmmm* or *aha!*—before the reader plunges back into the zone, but also that certain distractions might inspire a brief action related to the reading, like flipping back to the copyright page or forward to the author bio, or reading that confusing bit again.

To demonstrate an irrelevant bump, I tell about my experience with *Silent to the Bone* and the random, unproductive distractions I generated. My students volunteer similarly random and unproductive examples—the author mentions pizza and you wish you had a slice right now; a character's name is Reese and you visualize a peanut butter cup; the phrase *team spirit* makes you think of—and start to hum, oh, noooo—"Smells Like Teen Spirit." We agreed that the best response to these distractions is to treat them like flies and swat them away, so a reader can return to the zone ASAP.

The problem is that when we tell kids they have to seek connections as readers, we're teaching them to stop engaging in stories and start looking for distractions. And no one can be engaged and distracted at the same time. As Frank Smith observes, "When a book *grabs* us, we leave the everyday world around us and enter the world of the book. We are caught up in it. It is not possible to experience the world around us and the extended world of a book simultaneously. One always interferes with the other" (unpublished manuscript).

I tried to talk about all of this with a friend who's a proponent of comprehension strategies: how can it be productive to tell readers to distract themselves? He countered that once kids master and assimilate the strategies, they become automatic. And he assured me that I, too, had mastered the seven strategies, but so long ago—perhaps in some other lifetime?—that I'd forgotten acquiring this knowledge or putting it into practice. They, he said, are what account for my ability to enter the reading zone. And because my students lack my long history as a reader, they need me to teach them to do explicitly what I do unconsciously, in order to be able to read and understand stories as seamlessly as I do. He quoted the authors of *Mosaic of Thought*: "It may be that as we [adults] reintroduce ourselves to our own reading processes, we need to make conscious the strategies our minds have used subconsciously for so many years" (Keene & Zimmermann, 1997).

His argument brought to my mind the grammar teachers who are able to ignore a hundred years of careful research and tell me that the reason I don't consider grammatical structures when I speak or write is that I did such a good job of internalizing my elementary school teachers' prescriptions about syntax—how nouns come before verbs in English clauses—and thus produce these endless streams of sentences with all the words in the right order only because of grammar instruction I've forgotten.

This is an instance of what I've learned to describe as *magical thinking*. There isn't a shred of evidence that the study of grammar improves a child's abilities as a speaker or writer. Similarly, there is no evidence that grown-up, skilled, passionate, habitual, critical readers ever introduced ourselves to our cognitive strategies as readers of stories. From the time we first love stories and can enter the zone on our own, our reading processes—*unless we're distracted*—are unconscious, automatic, and, as Frank Smith describes them, "below the level of awareness" (1983). We don't think about how to comprehend as readers. We just do—unless we don't.

Comprehension is direct and unmediated. It is *the recognition of meaning.* When I see a poster that's an abstracted version of Shakespeare's first folio portrait, I don't say to myself, "Hmmm. I've seen that face before. I'll make a connection between my prior knowledge of images of this guy's face and the new schema created by the renderings of an abstract artist and recognize that this is intended as a modern representation of William Shakespeare." Instead, without a jot of metacognitive monitoring, I automatically make the meaning: *Shakespeare: cool.*

And when I can't comprehend something, even then the strategies are of limited value. For example, a friend included this sentence in a recent e-mail: "Just home from a quick dash to REI to replace lost Nalgenes." I was concerned—oh no, she lost her Nalgenes, this could be bad—but no matter how much comprehension strategizing I practiced, metacognitive processing was never going to clear up what a Nalgenes are. Or is. I had to ask. My husband didn't know either, but before he could Google it, our daughter and one of her outdoor-adventure-type friends rolled their eyes and explained about the cool water bottles you can buy at Recreational Equipment, Inc.

In other words, we comprehend what makes sense to us. One of the many virtues of frequent, voluminous reading is how it fills up the file drawers of long-term memory, increases our vicarious experience, and improves our comprehension of the world and the word. The more we read, the more that has the possibility of making sense to us, and the better we understand what we read.

But we cannot comprehend what makes no sense. And even then, we choose what we'll clear up and what we'll let pass: I still don't understand how batting averages are computed, so I just skip over the statistics when I read about the travails of the Red Sox. But I care about national politics, so I read that part of the front section of the *New York Times* every day, some articles twice, so I can be sure I understand. And I care about—and teach—literature and history, so I want to learn about them deeply enough that I can tantalize children, broaden their experience, and invite them to care, too.

So the issue becomes whether children can, or wish to, comprehend what they're being asked to read. It's estimated that a reader has to know, or be able to understand without too much effort, the meanings of about 90 percent of the words in a book, if comprehension is going to be possible (Carver, 2000). In other words, when children can't understand what they're reading, there's a strong possibility that the material is beyond them—that they can't figure out the meanings of enough of the words—not that they aren't activating appropriate comprehension strategies. This is the kind of reading selection that CTL teachers and students have learned to label as a Challenge, and the child who is struggling with it will need adult help in order to understand it.

But students who engage with self-selected, Just-Right stories *do* comprehend: they use what they know about syntax, semantics, and phonetics to figure out the few words they can't read and, otherwise, make meaning automatically, not to mention enthusiastically. In short, when individuals read stories they love in the reading workshop, and when the level of the writing falls within their abilities as readers, you cannot separate comprehension from reading. And, frankly, apart from a few days of standardized test prep, so kids can become familiar with the format, I'm hard put to justify any instructional context in which a K–8 reading teacher asks children to read stories they don't like or can't understand. Only readers who are bored, confused, or frustrated by a story will "need strategies" in order to comprehend it, and, even then, there are limits to what the strategies can fix or supply. Witness my experience with Nalgenes.

When I can't understand as a reader, I ask. I also reread, highlight, look things up in reference books or on the Internet, write notes to myself to try to work it out, or talk about the selection with someone else. Apart from packed texts such as poems, or archaic texts such as Shakespeare, my difficulties with understanding most often occur when I'm reading efferently, that is, not so much with novels or memoirs, but, more frequently, when it's an informational selection about history, science, current events, or education. I think that when teachers and students move beyond the stories of the reading workshop, to consider comprehension in the content-area disciplines, then, yes, indeed: it is appropriate, sensible, and helpful to talk about strategies for furthering one's understandings.

In addition to writing and reading, I teach seventh- and eighth-grade history and current events at CTL. My students' primary texts are volumes in *A History of US* by Joy Hakim (1993). I picked this series because it is lively, accurate, beautifully illustrated, packed with information, smart about causes and consequences, and written at about the fifth-grade level. In short, Hakim's writing style is inviting and accessible: my students immediately grasp at least 90 percent of the vocabulary, and when she uses language that's outside the experience of a typical kid reader, she stops to define it and give an example. Her informational prose is a model for social studies textbooks.

We supplement *A History of US* with readings from other trade books and textbooks, materials from the Jackdaw Press, and newspaper and journal articles. These texts are written at at least an eighth-grade reading level, and often higher. Sometimes my students need additional support to navigate them—listening to me read aloud, or getting together with partners or a small group to read, talk, and tease out salient information and theories.

I think at the middle school level and above, content-area specialists should be the teachers who take responsibility for helping students write and read the texts of their disciplines—this only makes sense. As their history teacher, it's my job to teach my students how to read the books and articles I assign in history class. For example, I show them how to preview a chapter from Hakim—how to skim it before they read it, note the headings, check out the illustrations, and establish a rough road map of the territory in their heads before they plunge in. Before I assign a homework reading, I read and synthesize it, then give kids specific information to seek, make sense of, and carry away from the assignment—for example, I've asked them to discover the three biggest myths about the "first" Thanksgiving, their own nominations for the top five reasons that Ben Franklin is an authentic American hero, their favorite delegate to the Second Continental Congress, the biggest idea about that winter in Valley Forge, or the reason they might want to say "thank you" the next time they meet a citizen of France.

Then, throughout the year, I teach history students how to read a selection twice, the first time to get the whole gestalt, and the second time with a pencil in hand to mark what seems to matter most, and I show them examples of my own highlighting and marginal notes. Here, too, we talk about noticing and monitoring the range of connections and distractions that are sure to pop up in their brainpans as they read history: are these blips relevant or random? And I do, in fact, teach some form of some of the strategies of proficient readers. In history class, where a reader's stance is most often efferent, asking questions, synthesizing new learning, and determining and focusing on what's important (Harvey &

Goudvis, 2002; 2003) are what reading and learning are all about. These are all effective *study skills*.

And this is the crux of the matter, when it comes to the comprehension-strategies approach. Some of its advocates posit that proficient readers use the seven strategies every time we read anything, whether it's "adults glued to a gripping novel or advanced placement seniors making their way through a physics text" (Keene & Zimmermann, 1997). But while I understand and appreciate that teachers *should* help students focus on their thinking when it's a physics text or a history article—so that kids may connect new knowledge to what they already know, understand events and phenomena, and react to them—when we return to the experience of reading stories in a reading workshop, we need to heed the warning of Louise Rosenblatt: "Do not use texts being read aesthetically for the explicit teaching of reading skills" (1980). Do not risk ruining the reading of stories by teaching children to focus on how they're processing them.

I began this chapter with an account of my experience as a teacher of comprehension strategies and a hunch about what attracted me to them in the first place: the belief—mistaken, as it turned out—that they loaned a rigor and structure that I feared my reading workshop lacked. I recognize that there are many teachers of reading who would describe their experiences with the strategies as positive. And I've wondered if what they most appreciate—as I did—is the tacit permission conveyed by this approach to teach reading with books, not basals.

However we may ask our students to process or respond to their reading, those of us who run any version of a reading workshop love children's trade books and the relationships we get to enjoy with our students through their literature. What I'm asking teachers to consider is whether a curriculum of study skills is the soundest way to help students become skilled, passionate, habitual, critical readers of the stories we—and they—adore. I recognize that this chapter will spark an occasion for cognitive dissonance in a reading teacher who believes in teaching the comprehension strategies, in a school district where this is the sanctioned approach to working with children and books. But I can't *not* raise issues about a method that I think distracts kids from experiencing the pleasures, the richness, and the depths of the reading zone.

Louise Rosenblatt once cautioned reading teachers about jumping on trends in methods. "Doing justice to the aesthetic mode of language behavior does not require discovery of a new array of teaching techniques," she observed (1980). Rather, it takes books that tell great stories and convey significant information in lively ways, and teachers who understand reading in both the aesthetic and efferent modes—what it feels like in the zone and how to invite kids to become immersed there, and, when students venture into prose that's primarily informational, what it's helpful to know and do so they're less likely to lose focus and more likely to learn facts. There is a time and place to pull the mechanics of reading comprehension out into the light and to parse them—again, in a history class or a science lesson or when unpacking a difficult poem. And then there are all those other moments with books when the story, the language, and the reader are all that matter.

In his beautiful, brilliant memoir of childhood reading, *The Child That Books Built* (2002), Francis Spufford almost captures the experience of comprehending stories in the reading zone. I qualify my appreciation with *almost* because this is how it must be. The processes of story reading are so subtle, so fantastic, so quicksilver and simultaneous, that we can't account for them, measure them, test them, or teach them. We can only give kids great books and time to get lost in them, then be grateful when a reader who writes as well as Spufford goes spelunking in the zone.

> In the meantime a child is sitting reading. Between the black lines of print and the eye, a channel is opening up through which information is pouring; more and faster than in any phone call, or any microcoded burst of data fired across the net, either, if you consider that these signals are not a sequence of numbers, not variations on a limited set of digital possibilities, but item after item of news from the analogue world of perception, each infinitely inflectable in tone and intent. The Prince sighs as his sick horse refuses to take sugar from his hand. Oatmeal sky over dank heather. It is a truth universally acknowledged that a man in possession of a fortune must be in want of a wife. Engage the star drive! Yet the receiving mind files away impression after impression. (Sometimes, to be sure, only in a mental container marked DON'T GET IT.) This heterogeneous traffic

leaves no outward trace. You cannot tell what is going on by looking at it: the child just sits there, with her book or his. It cannot be overheard, makes no incomprehensible chittering like the sound of a modem working on a telephone line. The subtlest microphone lowered into the line of transmission will detect nothing, retrieve nothing, from that incalculable flow of images (p. 22).

A fifth grader goes spelunking in Roald Dahl

CHAPTER 6

Booktalking

Trying to bring a book to life in a booktalk

I wasn't surprised when my students put book-talks at the top of the list of conditions essential to their engagement as readers—first, because they expend considerable effort trying to rip the featured titles out of my hands, sometimes before I can finish describing them, but more significantly, because about 90 percent of the titles students name in June as favorite reads of the school year were the subjects of booktalks, mine or theirs.

It isn't enough to fill a classroom with great titles. An important role of the reading teacher—the most important work, according to my students—is to become so intimate with good books that we bring life, with our voices, to the tattered spines that line the shelves of our libraries. We make it even more likely that kids will find books they love when students, too, have opportunities to inform their classmates about the titles that are too good to miss. So I learned to formalize the way I chat with an adult friend when I've finished a good book and want to share the wealth, and I brought that chat to the classroom in the form of a brief presentation called a booktalk.

My class of seventh and eighth graders and I conduct about three hundred booktalks each school year. This means that a student or I sit in the rocking chair for a minute or two and tell the story of a story we loved: who the main character is, what his or her problem is, a bit of the plot, maybe a theme of the book or its genre, what made the reader love it or how he or she read it, why it's a 9 or a 10, and, occasionally, why it's not.

Other than the book, there are no props or audiovisuals in a booktalk—no notes, either. Students let me know a day or so before they want to talk about a book, or I give a day's notice when I ask if a reader would be willing to booktalk a title he or she has just finished and rated highly. In the interim, student book-talkers can consider what they'll say about their books.

Booktalks are short, direct, and mostly enthusiastic: *endorsements* of particular titles, not oral reports. I learned early on, apart from the exceptions I've described below, not to promote a book that I can't rate as a 9 or 10 out of 10, and to ask my students to uphold the same standard. After a lukewarm review—even a 7 can be the kiss of death—a book will sit exactly where the booktalker put it down for the remainder of the school year.

I will break the endorsement rule when the purpose of a booktalk shifts from promotion to criticism—for example, the time I was disappointed with a young adult author's new book, or enraged by the conclusion of another novel, or puzzled by exactly what happened in a third. Then I'll tell kids, "This book surprised me or intrigued me, angered or flummoxed me, for these reasons. I'm not sure what to make of it. I can't even give it a rating. Does anyone else want to give it a try and see what you think?" Some of my kids' smartest writing about their reading is rooted in booktalks about titles that unsettled me, then unsettled—or satisfied—them.

I also break the endorsement rule when it's a new title that I haven't read yet. I explain to students what there is about the book that led me to buy it for our library, I read aloud the back or jacket-flap copy, and I ask who'd like to give it a try.

Because contests can break out among students over titles that sound especially attractive, I've learned to do the time-honored, fairest thing and ask anyone who wants the book next to raise his or her hand and guess the number I'm thinking. The closest guess gets the book first, and the others record the title on their "someday" pages.

At the start of a booktalk, mine or a student's, I ask everyone in the group to open his or her notebook to the someday page. However enthusiastic students may feel about a particular booktalked title, they're likely to forget about a book that sounded great on the day of the talk and to require more personalized headwork than I'm capable of, in the form of trying to invent answers for fifteen students in a class who'll ask, "I finished my book last night—what should I read next?" More important, kids need to learn how to function as independent, *intentional* readers—as readers with plans.

So I ask them to take responsibility for planning their reading. Each student bookmarks or dog-ears two pages in his or her reading notebook, titles them as "Someday Books," and records the titles and authors of intriguing books that a classmate or I booktalk. Then the reader tracks them down when he or she decides the time is right.

Finally, a crucial logistic of booktalking involves hinting at, but not revealing, the climax or resolution of a story. Most kids get this, but it doesn't hurt to point it out—or, if an essential plot point is about to be revealed by a student, to interrupt the booktalk: "Excuse me, I'm sorry, but do you really want to go there?"

Because I teach combined groups of seventh and eighth graders, in September some students are already familiar with a lot of the titles in our library. On the first day of school I meet with the eighth graders and schedule individuals to present talks about their favorite books. The September booktalks invite seventh graders into the community of middle-school book lovers, and they also begin to restock the books-we-love display, which I clear off over the summer. If I taught a single grade level—for example, just seventh—I'd begin the first trimester, and the books-we-love collection, with talks of my own about the titles that previous classes named as the best books.

I tend to booktalk several titles together, often in relationship to one another. Distinct categories of booktalks have emerged. In addition to *new titles I loved* and *new titles I haven't read yet*, there's *a worthy genre* (memoirs, free-verse novels and memoirs, dystopian sci-fi, humor and parody, antiwar novels, psychological mysteries, graphic journalism, and classics); *a worthy author* (a collection of books by one author, for example, Walter Dean Myers, Sarah Dessen, David Lubar, Pete Hautman, David Sedaris, Neil Gaiman, Ned Vizzini, Sonya Sones,

Booktalking a new favorite to the group

Barbara Kingsolver); *a worthy series* (His Dark Materials by Philip Pullman, Tomorrow When the War Began by John Marsden, Letters from a Nut by Ted L. Nancy, Abhorsen by Garth Nix); *oldies but goodies* (books copyrighted before 1995 that have stood the test of time with my kids, such as *The Outsiders, The Chocolate War, The Princess Bride, Don't Think Twice, Boy's Life, This Boy's Life, October Sky, Where the Red Fern Grows, Hoops, The Giver, Who Will Run the Frog Hospital?,* and *Say Goodnight, Gracie*); *titles related by topic or theme* (novels about athletes under pressure, vampires, censorship, peer pressure, girls in trouble, boys in trouble, teens figuring out who they are, gay and lesbian teens, friendship, family, survival); *top picks for the weekend*, which ensures that everyone has enough good books to carry him or her through until Monday; and *fast reads*, directed at struggling readers who are looking for intense action and for main characters whose motivations are unambiguous.

To illustrate how I promote books to a class of seventh and eighth graders, I've selected titles from three of the categories. In the first booktalk, I describe a title new to the classroom, *I Am the Messenger*, by the young Australian novelist Markus Zusak. Here, my goal is to convince students to take a chance on a brand-new book that I loved, by an author who none of them knows yet.

I loved *I Am the Messenger*. It took me about twenty pages to warm up to it, and then I was so hooked I read it in two days. It's a 10, for sure.

The main character is Ed Kennedy. He's nineteen and rootless—finished with school, hanging out with his friends and the world's smelliest dog, playing cards, failing to attract the girl he loves, living in a shack, driving a taxi to make ends meet. In the opening scene he surprises himself by foiling a bank robber, and he gets his picture in the local paper. And then playing cards start arriving—one at a time, all but one of them an ace—on which someone has written coded messages to Ed about people who need his help—missions that are sometimes violent, sometimes sweet, and that circle back in these odd but essential ways to Ed's life. Who's sending the cards and controlling his life? And why?

The answer is a total surprise. This is an ending you may need to read twice—like Cormier's *I Am the Cheese*—to appreciate it. Oh, and by the way, you'll want to turn the page and check out the photo of the author when you're done with the book. And I think I'm already on the verge of giving away too much.

I Am the Messenger is humorous, mysterious, contemporary realistic fiction—so funny in parts, especially the dialogue, that I laughed out loud. Markus Zusak is a great new writer—this is a name we need to keep an eye out for. There's genuine cleverness, character, *and* heart here. I've just started Zusak's latest, *The Book Thief*, and so far it's a 10, too.

Comments? Questions? Do I have any takers?

The subject of another of my booktalks is J. D. Salinger's *The Catcher in the Rye*. It's an oldie but goodie and not the easiest book to convince kids to give a fair shot these days. Some students abandon *Catcher* almost immediately, because Holden and his voice drive them crazy. So here I try to tempt them with the information that it's often banned, forewarn them about the complexity of Holden's personality, hint at the theme, and signify its importance to readers who are looking at the adult world and figuring out how they wish to grow up.

> It's been over fifty years since the publication of *The Catcher in the Rye*, and adults are still arguing about whether it's a classic novel about trying to come of age in an America of empty, phony values, or a disgusting novel that should be banned from American classrooms. I think it's a modern classic and a 10 for sure.
>
> The main character and narrator is Holden Caulfield. He's sixteen and miserable. He's just been kicked out of his high school—a prep school in Pennsylvania—and now he has to head home to New York City. But he's scared of confronting his parents, so he checks into a dive hotel instead, and for two days we follow his misadventures around Manhattan.
>
> Holden is an unforgettable teen character. He's complicated—funny and whiny, lonely and gregarious, sometimes obnoxious and sometimes compassionate, negative and nostalgic, and *obsessed* with the phoniness he sees everywhere. In other words, Holden may make you crazy at times, but Holden is worth it. The title refers to the one thing he can imagine he'd like to be when he grows up—I'll let you discover what it means.
>
> Some of what happens to Holden when he's loose in New York City is raw, and so is some of the language. But J. D. Salinger is writing here about the dark side of growing up—about one set of consequences of the fact that "Nothing Gold Can Stay," as Robert Frost put it. Please: do not leave your own adolescence behind without experiencing Holden's.
>
> Questions? Comments? Takers?

A third booktalk is directed at girl readers in general, and struggling girl readers in particular. The free-verse narratives of Sonya Sones are direct, packed, themed, and populated by unforgettable characters. Her work is a gift to teenaged girl readers.

Sonya Sones tells great stories about unforgettable teenaged girls in a unique style: her narratives are constructed of free-verse poems written in a first-person voice. Sones's free-verse memoir and novels are some of the most honest, intense, heartbreaking, humorous storytelling in our classroom library. I just love her.

Her first free-verse story, *Stop Pretending: What Happened When My Big Sister Went Crazy*, is autobiographical. When she was thirteen, her oldest sister suffered a psychotic break. She calls the main character *Cookie*, and these are Cookie's poems about her life after Sister is institutionalized—Cookie's visits to the psych ward and memories of times they shared in childhood, the impact on their parents, how her friends react when they find out, her fear of becoming "crazy," too, but also about finding her first love and wanting, more than anything, for Sister to "stop pretending"—stop the act and be who she used to be. There's an afterward by Sones in which she explains what happened to her sister and how this book came to be. *Stop Pretending* is about grief, resentment, guilt, shame, acceptance, and love. Unlike other autobiographical books about psychosis we've talked about—like *Girl, Interrupted* or *The Bell Jar*—this one focuses on someone who loves the "crazy" girl. It's remarkable—a 10 for certain.

Sones's next book, *What My Mother Doesn't Know*, is a straight-up, free-verse novel. The main character, Sophie, is almost fifteen, and the poems focus on her relationships with boys as she searches for The One. Sones is just great at capturing the intensity of love when you're a teen—and how fast the feelings can change. Lots of short poems allow Sophie to experience and tell about a lot—different boys, her friendships, her parents, being Jewish, being stalked, jealousy, puberty, kissing, fighting and making up, and Murphy, the guy at her school who no one but Sophie seems to see. *What My Mother Doesn't Know* is so honest and true about what it feels like to be fifteen and in love that it's scary—and a 10.

Sones's latest free-verse novel is *One of Those Hideous Books Where the Mother Dies*. It tells the story—in poems and, this time, e-mails, too —of Ruby, who's fifteen. When her mother dies, she has to leave Boston, her best friend, and her boyfriend, and fly to Los Angeles to live with her father. He and her mother divorced before Ruby was even born—she has never met him. And he just happens to be Whip Logan, one of America's most famous movie stars. Ruby's poems tell us what it's like to ride in a chauffeured limo, live in a mansion with Cameron Diaz as her next door neighbor, attend a high school full of the rich offspring of other celebrities, and feel homesick and lovesick, not to mention mistrustful and resentful of the glamorous stranger who's suddenly her father. This one is about grief and longing, love and divorce, and also about a secret and how trying to keep secrets in a family can hurt everyone. I gave it a 9.

Girls, my advice to you is to put Sonya Sones on your someday list. Do I have any takers?

In 2006, the Kids and Family Reading Report surveyed American child readers between the ages of five and seventeen and reported that almost a third of our middle school students, and almost half of fifteen-to-seventeen-year-olds, read only *two to three times a month*. The number-one reason kids cited for not reading more? They can't find books they want to read.

Classroom libraries of great, age-appropriate titles, along with heartfelt introductions to individual volumes, make books they *will* want to read visible to kids, not to mention available and attractive. And a personal record-keeping system like a someday page makes it easy to recall the titles that a reader craves.

Donald Graves once said that he thought a revealing measure of the effectiveness of a reading program or literature curriculum was whether students had plans as readers: ideas about what they want to read next or whom they want to read next. It's hard to make plans when you don't know what your options are. By briefing kids about the great stories that are still waiting for them, booktalks help students select, reject, develop criteria, look forward to the next title, and become the kinds of readers who can determine the course of a literary lifetime.

CHAPTER 7

One-to-One

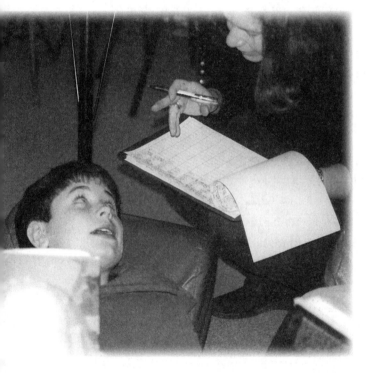

Checking in with readers and recording their progress

Striking a balance between lessons to the whole group and conversations with individual readers is a constant—and healthy, I've come to recognize—tension in my teaching. Some of what I know about books and reading has proved to be inspiring, thought-provoking, and useful to a class of readers, but sometimes what a student needs most isn't a rich discussion or a brilliant demonstration, but a one-to-one conversation about how things are going.

So I watch the length of my lessons and booktalks, so readers can read and I can talk with and teach them one at a time. Some conversations are out loud: when I circulate among my students and briefly bump each reader out of the zone by asking for just enough reflection to be able to monitor his or her progress and understandings. And some conversations are written down: when students have finished books, are interested in reflecting on them in depth, and, in collaboration with me or a friend, are ready to use writing to develop and refine their literary criteria.

The metaphor that has informed my vision of reading workshop, right from the start, is a dining room table—my dining room table, around which my family and friends talk easily and often about the books we're reading. I'm on a never-ending quest to get that table into my classroom, so my students and I can deliberate, defend, rhapsodize, reconsider, teach, and learn around it, as readers do. If reading workshop is the table, its legs are daily chats with individual readers and occasional letters, back and forth, about books and authors,

In the 1980s, intrigued by the dialogue-journal research of Jana Staton (1980), I initiated written-down conversations about their reading to help my students—and myself—reflect about books in a way that isn't possible with talk. Twenty-five years later, I'm still corresponding with middle school kids about books and still tinkering with the approach—revising the procedures and restructuring the dialogues so they're ever more authentic, productive, and manageable.

I know that, inspired by my book *In the Middle* (1987, 1998), other teachers initiated literary correspondence too, but at a cost. The paper load—written exchanges about books with every student every week—is exhausting. Exhausted myself, I cut my paper load in half by asking students to alternate their letters in cycles: three exchanges back and forth with me, then three back and forth with one classmate of their choosing.

This adaptation made my teaching life more manageable, but it didn't resolve another problem with the weekly letters: sometimes my students didn't have a lot to say about their reading. A reader might have started a memoir just prior to the journal deadline, and it was too soon to write about it, except in the most perfunctory way. Or a reader might remain engrossed in a fat, fantasy novel from one week to the next and, apart from the latest plot development, have nothing new to say. Or a reader might be in the thick of a good story, at a point where it's inappropriate—if not undesirable, if not impossible—to detach from the zone and consider an author's choices.

The best letters, always, seemed to come after a student had finished a book. These responses were extended, engaged, referred specifically to the text and what the author had done, described reactions to whole works, and, in general, functioned as literary criticism—informal and tentative, yes, but still *critical*, in all the best senses of the word.

So I went back to the drawing board. The latest incarnation of literary letters in my classroom takes the form of *letter-essays* that students write to me or a classmate every three weeks about books they have finished reading. These are first-draft-finals, informal and unrevised. A September invitation to students establishes the contents and procedures:

10 September

Dear _____,

Your reading journal is a place for you, me, and your friends to consider books, reading, authors, and writing. You'll think about your books in informal essays directed to me and friends, and we'll write back to you about your ideas and observations. Our letter-essays and responses will become a record of the reading, thinking, learning, and teaching we accomplished together.

Each letter-essay should be at least two pages long and written as a personal, critical response to one book—in other words, not a series of paragraphs about a series of books, but a long look at one that intrigues you. You should write a letter-essay to me or a friend in your own journal every three weeks, due on Thursday mornings. We'll correspond in cycles: you'll write two letter-essays to me, then two to a friend of your choosing.

Before you write, look back over your reading record. Which title that you've finished would be most enjoyable to revisit as a fan? What book that you abandoned—or remained hopeful about to the bitter end—would be most enjoyable to revisit in a slam? Once you've decided, return to the book. Skim it, and select at least one passage you think is significant, in terms of how you reacted to the book's theme, problem, character development, or plot arc, or to the author's style. Choose a chunk of text that you think *shows something essential*. In your letter-essay, quote—*copy*—the passage you chose, and write about what you think it shows about the book, the author, or your response to either.

What else might you do in a letter-essay? Tell about your experience as a reader of the book. Describe what you noticed about how the author wrote. Tell what you think the themes might be. Tell what surprised you. Pose your wonderings—your questions about the author, the characters, the structure, the voice, and yourself as a reader. Try the sentence openers [see page 83] I provided to help get you thinking and writing. *Be aware that a good letter-essay is one that teaches you something you didn't realize about your book, or yourself as a reader, before you wrote it.*

Once you've written your letter, hand-deliver your journal to your correspondent. If that's me, please put it in my rocking chair on Thursday morning. When a friend gives you his or her journal, you should answer, in at least paragraph length, by Monday morning. After you've written back, hand-deliver your friend's journal—don't put it in his or her locker or backpack. You may not lose or damage another's reading journal.

Date your letter-essays in the upper right-hand corner, and use a conventional greeting (*Dear* _____ ,) and closing (*Love, Your friend, Sincerely,*). Always cite the name of the author of the book and its title. Indicate the title by capitalizing and underlining it—for example, The Outsiders by S. E. Hinton.

I can't wait for us to begin reading and thinking about literature together in this serious-but-friendly way. I can't wait for your first letter-essays and a year of chances to learn from you, learn with you, and help you learn more about the power and pleasures of books.

Love,

Nancie

I trim photocopies of the letter so it fits within a marble composition book. In an early September mini-lesson, students glue it inside the front covers of their reading journals and highlight it as I read it aloud. I also give them a copy of a letter-essay that I drafted, to demonstrate what I'm asking of them. And because I can't write anything without pre-seeing it—even my lists begin in lists—I show kids a planning page (Atwell, 2002) I made (see Fig. 7-1 below) before I drafted my letter-essay (see page 79). Some students find this to be a useful technique before they write about their reading, while others are able to just plunge in.

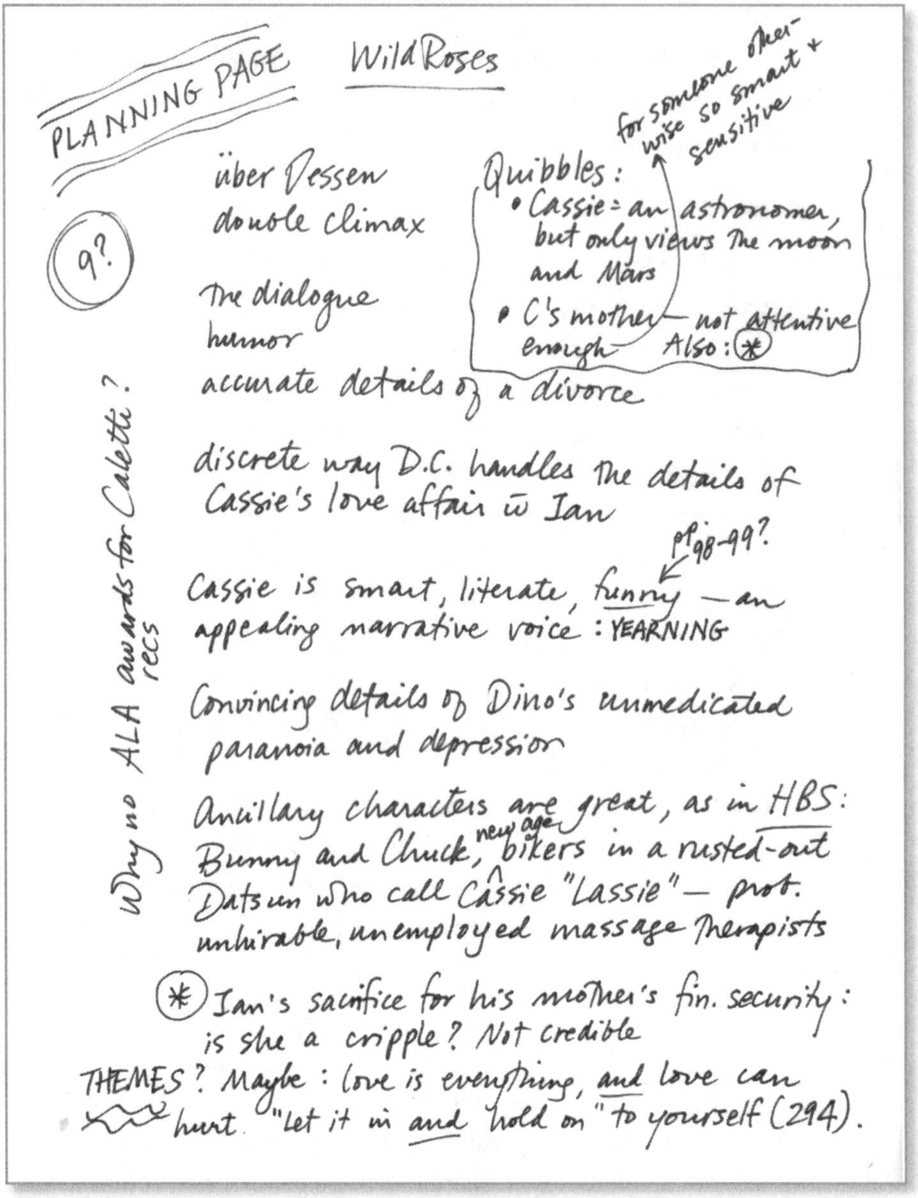
PLANNING PAGE

Wild Roses

über Dessen

double climax

9?

The dialogue

humor

accurate details of a divorce

discrete way D.C. handles the details of Cassie's love affair w Ian

Cassie is smart, literate, funny — an appealing narrative voice : YEARNING

pp 98-99?

Convincing details of Dino's unmedicated paranoia and depression

Ancillary characters are great, as in HBS: Bunny and Chuck, new age bikers in a rusted-out Datsun who call Cassie "Lassie" — prob. unhirable, unemployed massage therapists

(*) Ian's sacrifice for his mother's fin. security: is she a cripple? Not credible

THEMES? Maybe : love is everything, and love can hurt. "Let it in and hold on" to yourself (294).

Quibbles:

• Cassie = an astronomer, but only views the moon and Mars

for someone other-wise so smart + sensitive

• C's mother — not attentive enough

Also: (*)

Why no ALA awards for Caletti? recs

FIGURE 7-1 *My pre-letter-essay notes about the novel* Wild Roses

3 September

Dear Gang of Readers,

Deb Caletti is a new favorite young adult author of mine. Although the title doesn't fit the story, *Wild Roses* is still a 9. To begin with, the problem is interesting and different: Cassie Morgan's mother, a cellist, leaves Cassie's father for Dino, a world-famous violinist and composer, and marries him. Dino is eccentric in the extreme, if not psychotic. And Cassie falls in love with Dino's student, Ian. There are two climaxes, and the resolution, although a kind of happy ending, is also the source of one of my quibbles about the novel, which is definitely contemporary realism.

I'd compare Caletti to Sarah Dessen, because of her character development. Cassie resembles Dessen's girl main characters in that she's smart, articulate, literate, contemplative, passionate—she *yearns*, as Dessen's girls do—and funny. The narrative voice is first person, and Cassie's voice is smart, observant, and appealing. Here's an example.

> I was going through life in a fog, an expression that was true in every sense. I felt like I was watching and not really participating, like my life source had called in sick and was wrapped up in a quilt somewhere, zonked on cold medicine. And the fog was a literal truth, too—for those days it lay around me in wispy streams, around the water and on the lawn in the morning, as if the clouds had pushed the wrong elevator button. That's what fog is anyway—lazy clouds. Clouds without ambition. The fog was eerie and beautiful, soft and thoughtful, and it usually lifted in the afternoon to an annoying display of sun that made the October orange colors so bright they hurt your eyes. Everything glistened with dew, and it was vibrantly cold out. I didn't want that, the cold that made you want to put on a big coat and do something useful and happy, like rake leaves. I wanted the rain again, or just the fog, looking miserable and spooky.
>
> I went through the motions at school, caring even less than usual about the fact that Kileigh Jensen highlighted her hair or that rumors were flying about what Courtney did with Trevor

Woodhouse, which everyone knew anyway by taking one look at them. The things that I might have laughed at, the fact that Sarah Frazier wore enough makeup for her and two of her closest friends, for example, or the coincidence that Hailey Barton's bra size doubled right about the time that two Chihuahuas disappeared from the area, didn't even seem funny (pp. 98–99).

I think this is an effective mix of self-awareness, sensory description, and humor. It's typical of the voice and persona that Caletti invents for Cassie. I'm surprised that neither *Wild Roses* nor Caletti's first two novels, *Honey, Baby, Sweetheart* and *The Queen of Everything*, aren't ALA recommended titles. Caletti's should be a name middle school teachers—and kids—know better.

I like her dialogue. A lot of it comes out of left field, especially the voices of Nannie, Cassie's senile but crafty grandmother, and Bunny and Chuck, two overweight, New Age bikers without bikes who ride around in a rusted-out Datsun, call Cassie "Lassie," and wonder why they can't get jobs in their chosen field, which is massage therapy.

Much of the plot development felt convincing to me: the details of Cassie's parents' divorce and custody arrangement; the description of how Dino spirals down into depression and paranoia when he stops taking the psychotropic drugs that impede his creativity; and the love affair between Cassie and Ian, which not only rings true but also has a curtain drawn across it by Cassie/Caletti in a way that's more romantic than the usual details of physical relationships in most YA fiction.

I do have plot issues: as part of Cassie's character development, Caletti gives her an interest/expertise in astronomy, but the two times we see Cassie with a telescope, she's viewing the moon and Mars—obvious choices, and with no details or vocabulary to convince us that Cassie is serious.

And then there are the mothers. Cassie's doesn't pay attention to her, but this isn't presented as a problem from the perspective of a sensitive teenaged girl. And Ian's mother's financial security seems to hinge on her teenaged son becoming a world-famous concert violinist. Since she's able-bodied, I don't get it. It feels as if Caletti might have spent more time thinking through these relationships and motivations.

As for its theme, I think *Wild Roses* is about the power of love—love of others *and* of self. Caletti has Cassie discover that even though love causes pain, she has to "let it in, but hold on" to herself in the process (p. 294). The concluding section, in which Cassie comes to this understanding, is especially well written.

I'm looking forward to whatever else Deb Caletti writes next, on the basis of the girl main characters she has created so far.

Love,

Nancie

My hunch was that occasional letter-essays, as opposed to weekly correspondence about their reading, would be both more demanding and more forgiving for my students. By asking them to think critically and at length about one book, I hoped they would go deeper as critics. I also guessed that looking back and choosing *the one* story they wanted to write about would enhance their engagement and sharpen the writing. And, finally, because writing about one's thinking makes people smarter in general, I hoped that thinking and writing about whole books would help the kids become smarter about literature in particular.

My students confirmed my hunches, and more. In November I asked them, as part of the first-trimester reading self-evaluation, "How are the letter-essays working for you?" As these excerpts demonstrate, their responses were thoughtful and overwhelmingly positive.

I enjoy them a lot more than our original, weekly reading journals. They are more in-depth, so I can say <u>everything</u> I want to say about one book.

• ◆ •

It is easier and more interesting to be able to write about any book that I've read, rather than the one I happen to be reading at the moment.

• ◆ •

I enjoy the letter-essays because I recognize things in the writing that I didn't when I first read it, such as an author's techniques for character development. I also enjoy putting a passage from the book in my letter, so my correspondent knows what I'm writing about, and I do, too.

• ◆ •

I feel more like a critic this way, telling what I think the author did well or could have done better.

· ◈ ·

I've noticed a lot more about myself as a reader, about my process and my preferences.

· ◈ ·

Now I like seeing what the person who writes to me thinks of a book, because they go deeper than they used to go in every-week letters.

· ◈ ·

To me, they are a way to let out <u>all</u> my feelings about a book. I don't realize how much I have to say until I start writing.

· ◈ ·

I feel proud of myself when I've written so well about a book that I hook one of my friends on it.

· ◈ ·

The openers force me to be more analytical and to generally <u>think</u> more in response to literature, and the letters prepare us for high school and college essays about books.

The last comment, written by my student Lincoln, refers to another rationale for the letter-essays: in high school to some extent, but in college for sure, my students will write critical papers about literary texts in which they develop arguments founded on evidence that they provide—references to an author's techniques and themes, accompanied by pertinent quotations from the text. So I also viewed the letter-essays as a bridge between the chatty letters about their reading that CTL students of grades 1–4 continue to write every week—and kids in grades 5–6 every other week—and the longer, more formal analyses that young adults and adults craft about our reading.

In his response, above, Lincoln mentions how "the openers" have made him more analytical when he writes about his reading. He's referring to a one-page list (see page 83) I devised to help kids begin to take a spectator role as readers—to exit the zone and stand apart from a literary work they loved, hated, or aren't sure of, then to focus on their own response *and* on what an author did to engender it. I photocopy this handout on brightly colored bond and trim it so it, too, fits inside a marble composition notebook. My kids use it to bookmark their journals, and they consult it for ideas of what they might say next about their books.

Writing About Reading: Some Openers

I was surprised when/angry about/satisfied with/moved by/incredulous at/. . .

I liked the way the author

I noticed how the author

I don't get why the author

If I were the author I would have

I'd compare this author to

This book reminded me of

The main character

The character development

The narrative voice

The structure of this book

The climax of the plot

The resolution of the main character's problem

The genre of this book

I'd say a theme of this book is

I wish that

I didn't agree with

I understood

I couldn't understand

Why did

This is how I read this book:

I rated this one _____ because

And always: I was struck by/interested in/convinced by this passage: ". . ."
It shows . . . about this author's writing.

My students' letter-essays are deeper, more interesting to read, and easier to respond to than weekly entries. Now they have a lot to say, and so do I. In my responses, I try to react to their reactions, as both a teacher and a reader. This means I affirm or challenge their insights, describe my own experiences and opinions, offer suggestions, present arguments, make recommendations, and provide background information. For example, in my first exchange with Nathaniel, a seventh grader, I floated a theory; made a book recommendation, which he followed up on; and offered some direction for his next letter-essay.

Sept. 25

Dear Nancie,

The Game of Sunken Places is one of my favorite fantasy novels. Most other authors would have probably made this story muddled and confusing, due to its unique topic, but M. T. Anderson's quick, to-the-point writing made it an extremely amusing and fast-paced book. Unlike other novels I have read recently, I was involved in the story almost immediately.

Greg and Brian are the main characters in this book. Their problem is that Greg's mysterious uncle invited him and a friend (Brian) to come and visit. When they get to their rooms, they find the Game of Sunken Places. It is an old board game that is an exact replica of the mansion that they are staying in. When they figure out that they are actually *in* the game, and that two "spirit-nations" are betting on who will win it, they become determined to beat their mysterious opponent.

> "Two spirit-nations are at war. You will decide the conflict. On the one side, there are the People of the Mound of Norumbega, who used to live here. On the other side, the Thusser Hordes, who drove them out." Uncle Max bowed his head against the headrest of the chair.
> Gregory demanded, "What happens if we lose?"
> "A treaty was struck," said Uncle Max. "The People of Norumbega were forced into exile. But there is a chance for return. The Game is arranged. Rounds are played. If the Norumbegans win, they will return from their exile. If the Thusser

Hordes win, they will take possession of the mountain, the Mound of Norumbega."

Brian was incredulous. "The fate of this whole spirit-nation depends on whether we win or lose?"

I thought it was an interesting choice Anderson made to change the main character as the book progressed—at first Gregory is the main character, but then Brian begins to slowly take that position. The book is in third person (e.g., "Greg jumped") so the change is not *that* drastic.

This novel is a combination of fantasy, adventure, and a bit of realistic fiction because most of it could be real, but some parts are fantasy. The only problem I had about *The Game of Sunken Places* was that I found the climax to be a little fast. I think that with the entire plot building up to it, more could have come of it. Because of that, I would rate this an 8.5, not a 9 or a 9.5.

If I had to decide one theme for this book, it would be friendship, because that is what is holding G and B together the entire story. In the end (I know I shouldn't normally do this, but I also know that you have read it) Gregory gives up all the glory and lets Brian become the hero. They worked as friends to win the game for the good side. Then, when they figured out that they were supposed to be opponents, Gregory lets himself lose for the better good.

Overall, I think this book is a great read.

Sincerely,
Nathaniel

30 September

Dear Nathaniel,

I agree with you: the character development was different. At first it bothered me—Greg and Brian seemed more like cardboard cutouts than real boys. But I hung in there because I've learned to respect and trust Anderson's writing, and I think I figured out—maybe—what he's up to.

Have you ever read or heard of the Hardy Boys books? It was a series started by Edward Stratemeyer in the early 1900s, with a heavy emphasis on adventures and solving mysteries but with zero character development. Stratemeyer also created Tom Swift and Nancy Drew, two other one-dimensional adventure-series heroes.

I think Anderson updated the Hardy Boys tradition in *Game of Sunken Places*—and beautifully. His style is clean and fluid, and his plotting is intriguing. I'd read anything he wrote, simply out of curiosity about what he was up to next, style- and theme-wise. He's definitely an experimenter.

Have you tried Anderson's *Feed* yet? It's terrific.

Love,

Nancie

P.S. Thanel, although the passage you excerpted does move the plot, your comments about it don't illustrate anything essential about Anderson's style or the theme of *GSP*. Next time you write, please choose a chunk of text that you think is significant in terms of the author's style, themes, character development, etc. It's more than okay to be selective and specific when you gloss a quotation.

In my responses to their letter-essays, I try to help students focus on the author's craft and their responses to what the author crafted—to notice how a book made them feel and how a writer achieved the effect—and to take a stance that's both personal and critical. I want kids to go beyond plot and personal associations and to begin to make observations and decisions about what is and isn't working in pieces of their reading. Giving students time, distance, and a safe context allows them to use writing as a way to *think* about literature. In this exchange with Grace, an eighth grader, we collaborated to notice the character development in Elizabeth Berg's *Durable Goods* and to consider the Berg oeuvre.

3/28

Dear Nancie,

Recently I read *Durable Goods* by Elizabeth Berg. I rated it a 9 or 10 in comparison to her other book, *Talk Before Sleep*.

I really like the lead because the main character, Katie, does some-thing bad, so Elizabeth Berg makes the reader want to know what will happen. I think that is effective because we (the readers) start right into the action, so it's pretty hard to put the book down.

I thought the father was very realistic, and so was the impact of Katie's mother's death before the book starts. The father was realistic because he wasn't the predictable "mean dad who hits his daughters." He had a sensitive side to him that, for the most part, only Katie could see.

The impact of the mother's death was realistic because there were little quirks that Katie did, such as when she was sad, she would take us back into a time in her past where she and her mother were talking or laughing. Katie also had a spot under her bed where she would go when she was sad or confused, and she would just talk to her mother as if she was really there. I think that was a good thing Katie did, because when people are sad or confused, everyone urges them to "talk about it," which Katie does. I think that was very smart.

The structure of the book towards the end confused me at first because Katie, her big sister, and her sister's boyfriend run away. So Elizabeth Berg makes us feel like Katie will start her new life with them. But instead, the conclusion switches to Katie going back home to her dad, alone, and starting her new life with *him*. I thought that was smart of Elizabeth Berg, because if the book ended with Katie running away, with this terrible past, she couldn't have changed her past into a new future, which she ended up doing, if that makes any sense. This passage resonated for me:

> I can have a puppy. I can have a boyfriend. I can have a good husband, live in a house with him. I go into the living room, think how I'd decorate it. Well, curtains, for one thing; it is only civilized. And something baking in the oven, to make smells you can almost hold. Some plants. Some pictures we would pick out together: "Do you like that one?" "Well, of course, if you do, dear." Yes, and an ashtray for guests who smoke, and a candy dish, all with wrapped-up toffees.

I liked this passage because it seemed like throughout the whole book, Katie was comparing her real lifestyle to the one in her imagination, and yet she makes so much out of this one year of her life. I think Elizabeth

Berg created Katie as a role model for all girls, especially ages 12 to 14, so I would recommend this book to every girl in our class.

I can't wait to read *Joy School* by Elizabeth Berg, which is the sequel to *Durable Goods*. I hope it is just as good. I also want to start an Elizabeth Berg theme, just as I had a Sarah Dessen theme. Can you recommend some of Berg's best?

Love,
Grace

29 March

Dear Grace,

I think that Berg, unlike Dessen, is an uneven writer. I've had a hard time enjoying—believing in/caring about—about half of her novels. For me, the worthwhile titles are *Durable Goods*, *Joy School*, *Talk Before Sleep*, and *Range of Motion*. I found everything else to be surprisingly bad in terms of plot, voice, but mostly character motivation and plausibility. I can't think of a writer who has so moved *and* so disappointed me.

I spotted a new Berg in hardcover at the bookstore today and was tempted to buy it, then decided to let someone at the *NYTBR* weigh in first, because I felt so burned by her last few novels.

Katie is one of my favorite girl characters in modern literature: right up there with Scout and the narrator of *I Capture the Castle*. Her voice is authentic, expressive, and *true*. The passage you chose is the essence of her age and personality—as you observed, full of daydreams but wide-eyed, too. Katie is Berg's triumph as a writer. I think you'll love *Joy School*.

Love,
Nancie

The dozen or so exchanges in each student's reading journal, over the course of a school year, are opinionated, reflective, literary discourse. In contrast, our daily, face-to-face conversations provide a context for the essential chat that keeps young readers reading, thinking, planning, *in the zone*. It also follows up on, and extends, what I learn and what they learn through the dialogues in the journals.

Reading Conferences

Left: A kindergartner reads to his teacher, Helene Coffin

Bottom: A first grader confers with Ted DeMille about Dinotopia

Right: Glenn Powers helps a fifth grader find her next Just Right

Bottom: A seventh grader and I chat about a favorite author

It took me a while to learn how to chat. Without the time to reflect that writing gives me, I didn't always know what was helpful or important to say to a reader. So I'd ask, "What's your book about?" and get, in response, an endless plot summary that kept me from talking with more than a few kids each class period. More significantly, these conferences didn't offer students help, support, or direction, which should be the heart of any teaching conversation.

What I *should* know about my kids as readers, day to day, is whether they're okay: Are they understanding what they're reading? Happy with it? In the reading zone? In need of advice or information from me? So I began to concentrate on a couple of open-ended questions—"What do you think so far?" or "How is it?" When they began to tell me about their experiences as readers of books, then I was able to follow up with observations or questions that sustained my students as readers, unburdened them, and taught them.

Some of the concepts and language that inform our conversations in reading workshop have their roots in writing workshop, in my lessons about narrative voice, plot structure, pace, and character development. Other questions help kids articulate their literary criteria. Sometimes I ask readers to venture a tentative assessment of an author's choices, or I'll rescue readers who haven't been able to immerse in the zone—who need a different book, or a strategy to untangle themselves. Some queries help readers to make plans. And one checks up on homework reading: *What page are you on today?* A question I never ask explicitly, although it involves a subject that's often implicit in our conversations, is "What's the theme of this book?" I've learned that readers can only know for certain about the ideas that will emerge from a story after the whole thing has had time to settle inside them.

Literacy educator Margaret Meek wrote, "For all the reading research we have financed, we are certain only that good readers pick their own way to literacy in the company of friends who encourage and sustain them and that . . . the enthusiasm of a trusted adult can make the difference" (1982).

Some Questions I Ask as I Roam Among Readers

Always:

What page are you on?

Mostly:

What do you think so far?

How is it?

What's happening now?

And also:

Any surprises so far?

How did you feel when you got to the part about _____?

Main character queries:

Who's the main character in this one?

What's the main character like?

What's his problem, or hers?

How's the character development in general? Are you convinced?

Author queries:

Who wrote this one?

What do you think of the writing so far?

Do you know anything about the author?

Any theories about why he or she might have written this?

How is it so far, compared to his or her other books?

Critical queries:

What genre is this one?

How is it so far, compared with other books about _____?

Is it plausible?

How's the pace?

What's the narrative voice? How's that working for you?

What do you think of the dialogue/format/length of chapters/flashbacks/ inclusion of poems/diction choices/author's experiments with _____, and so on (depending on the book)?

When it's a page-turner:

What's making this a page-turner for you, vs. a literary novel? What are you noticing? For example, is it formulaic—easy for you to predict?

Process queries:

Why did you decide to read this one?

I can't believe how much you read last night. Tell me about that.

Why did you decide to reread this one?

Where did you find this book?

When there's no zone:

Is this book taking you into the reading zone?

Why do you think it's taking you so long to read this?

Can you skim the parts that drag—the descriptions, for example?

Are you confused because it's hard to understand the language, or because you can't tell what's going on?

Are you considering abandoning this book? Because if you're not hooked by now, that's more than okay. You can always come back to it someday.

Do you want to skim to find out what happens, or even read just the ending, then move on to a better book?

What's on your someday list?

Do you know what other book I think you might like?

Finis:

Now that you've finished it, what will you rate this one?

Is this one worthy of a booktalk? Do you want to schedule a talk for tomorrow?

What are you planning to read next?

Now there's a scope and sequence that just makes sense. Teach reading so that student readers feel *the enthusiasm of a trusted adult* when we communicate to them one-to-one about literature—so they get that the teacher loves books, and that our advice about reading them is trustworthy. And invite every student to become part of a community of readers, one of a *company of friends who encourage and sustain one another.* The dining room table is huge. It has to be. There is room enough around it for every student to pull up a chair and feel encouraged and sustained.

CHAPTER 8

Boys

Guys: They can fix cars and love a good story

I can't believe I'm titling something with the name of a gender, but here we are. As a teacher who writes about teaching, my topic for the past twenty-five years has been *kids* and how to help them, girls and boys, become skilled, passionate, habitual, critical readers and writers.

But then the boy industry coalesced and announced the boy crisis. In spite of strong evidence to the contrary derived from comparisons of years of NAEP and SAT scores (see Mead, 2006), the boy industry claims that the educational achievement of young males is in decline because American schools are neglecting guys. The rise of girls' scores over this same period gave birth to a couple of convenient myths. One is that expanded educational opportunities for women, starting in the 1970s with the passage of Title IX, came at the expense of progress for boys. Another is that teachers, in a profession dominated by females, tend to choose girl-friendlier methods and materials, approaches that discriminate against masculine interests, personalities, and styles of learning.

In the arena of the language arts, the arguments and evidence for a boy crisis are rich in stereotypes, about boys in general and boy readers in particular, to wit:

- Boys perceive books as isolating, unnatural, and antisocial.

- Boys find it difficult to imagine fictional worlds.

- Boys are unable to engage with writing that describes complex emotions and relationships.

- Boys are drawn to nonfiction because it's practical, while novels aren't.

- Boys need comics, magazines, sports pages, gaming guides, and *The Guinness Book of Records*, because of their shorter attention spans.

- Boy culture regards reading as a sissy thing.

- Boys are born competitors and kinetic learners, so a passive experience such as reading a book thwarts their nature.

- And even, get this one, boys' brains have less neuron density in the temporal lobe cortex, which is associated with verbal ability, so genetic differences put males at a disadvantage when it comes to reading.

I read the essays, articles, and books about the boy crisis, and I shake my head. *Who are these boys?* I cannot recognize a single one of the guys I teach in the stereotypes. And I teach *guys*.

My male students hunt with their fathers and uncles. They play basketball, baseball, and soccer, domesticate rats and ferrets, play disgusting practical jokes, master Magic Cards, drive ATVs illegally, bait and haul lobster traps, blow things up, play computer games for twelve hours straight, haunt the video arcade at the Portland mall, watch *The Simpsons* and *South Park*, live for hip-hop *or* heavy metal, and collect roadkill and freeze it for use in future "experiments." And they read books. And they love books.

Anyone's achievement, male or female, is driven by interest. Give boys stories and main characters that grip them, and they will read books with passion. Give them a boring, inaccessible curriculum of assigned readings from textbook anthologies and the novels of the American secondary school canon, and they will dread reading just as much as I did when I was in middle and high school.

When boys *and girls* choose their own books, when teachers make it our business to put the right story into every reader's hand, and when we create quiet, comfortable spaces in kids' lives for them to enjoy books on a regular and predictable basis, then every student can enter the reading zone, and no one ever thinks in terms of testosterone or neuron density.

As a teacher who writes about teaching and learning, some of my best evidence takes the form of stories about students. I hope that a brief sketch of one of the guys—Cameron—will help dispel the myth of the boy reader.

Cam was my student for two years. His dad works construction and drives a plow truck, and his mom cleans homes. He is an athlete, a competitor, and a demon for speed. He's become a champion tennis player and a Babe Ruth All-Star. He just traded up to a more powerful dirt bike— eighty cc's—and he likes to spend a Sunday afternoon in Greene, Maine, watching the motorcycle races and dreaming of the day he'll be out there on the track himself. Cam, his friends, and his brother have even invented sports, including golf-kind-of, medium-contact soccer, and extreme sledding, which he described in a memoir (see page 97).

In addition to his sledding vignette, written for the class yearbook, Cam finished two other memoirs as an eighth grader, plus a lot of free-verse poetry, an essay about the dangers of radon gas, a letter of application, a movie review, and a short story about a boy who watches, fears, and finally confronts two friends who bully other kids. Cam concluded the speech he delivered at his CTL graduation with "Volcanic Activity in My Backyard," a poem that—in its subject matter, tone of nostalgia, sense of humor, sensory details, and theme—shows a lot about who he is, as a boy standing on the cusp of adulthood. I've included the poem on page 98. I think it's the essence of Cameron.

Cam is a guy, but he is no stereotype of a boy. He uses his literacy to help him measure the distance between who he once was, who he is now, and who he might become. I predict that someday he'll become a great husband, father, and

Extreme Sledding

by Cameron Blake

I push my way into the recess mob huddled near the math/science room door and make my way to the front of the pack. Hands rest eagerly on the cold metal handle of the door as we resist the urge to burst out into the warm spring air. Finally, after what seems like hours, the helping teacher shows up and releases us into recess.

Immediately a chunk of the group, me included, races towards the grey metal shed. I spin around the corner and slide open the rusty doors. We each snatch a sled from the pile—unusual anywhere else in America in the month of May—then run down the narrow pathway to the barn.

Once there, we survey the steep slope behind the barn and inspect our previous trails down the grass-covered hill. Tracks from yesterday, still visible from the top, seem intact. Kids begin to scramble to the nearest available run, and I find myself waiting in line on the middle track.

Finally the line has disappeared. I stand at the edge of the trail, visualizing my run. The kid behind me shouts for me to hurry up, and I quickly hop on my sled and take the position.

Now, I lean forward and push off with my feet, sending me down the initial slope. I begin slowly at first, catching on the rough gravel, but then gain speed once I hit the matted-down grass. I tear down the slope and maneuver my way through the various rocks, bumps, holes, and whatever else stands between me and the bottom of the hill.

I'm halfway down when I hit a lump of dirt, which sends my sled careening off course, veering into the other trails. I clip the back of Steven's sled, sending him off course as well. Luckily, we hit square on.

I flip sideways and fly off my sled. I tumble down the hill, seeing green, blue, green, blue, green, blue, then the final green as I crash at the bottom. I lie flat on my stomach for a moment and notice Steven, who's just starting back up the trail.

I jog over and grab my sled, now tossed off to the side, and trudge back up the steep hill. I reach the top and jump back in line. I continue to ride down the steep incline, run after run, mostly to end up mashed into the ground at the bottom.

When the bell rings, I groan and start walking towards the school, my clothes covered with grass stains. As I toss my battered sled into the pile in the shed, I begin to wonder what my mom will think of my pants, now almost solid green, when she sees them. But my moment of worry evaporates as soon as Nancy T. calls us over from the coat area to begin the kindergarten read-aloud.

This sport lasted many recesses and all year round, becoming most dangerous of all on the ice of winter. I think back now and can't imagine how sliding down that hill, on grass or ice, could have given us so much fun, no matter how many times we traversed it, courtesy of our trusty, plastic sleds.

Volcanic Activity in My Backyard

by Cameron Blake

I grab the brown handle
and climb the wooden rings.
I'm elected to go first,
so I reel in the first swing
that dangles over the molten
    lava.

I find the best grip,
brace myself, and hop off the
    ledge.
I swoop down,
clinging for dear life until I
    have settled,
then stand with one foot
    on the melting rubber
    seat.

There's no turning back now.

Carefully I step onto the final
    swing.
Halfway there.
Then I reach *them*, the
    dreaded rings,
which have often seen the
    last of me
(until the next day)
as I plunge into the orange
    and red sea of heat.

I stretch my arm out,
w a y out, until I've
    almost fallen off.
Useless.

So then I begin to swing,
shifting my weight
side to side to side to side
until I have swung just far
    enough
to grasp the plastic doughnut.

Quickly I leap off the last
    swing,
cling onto the second ring,
and lift my feet as high as I
    can.
It's too late.
My loose sneaker brushes
    the burning surface
and drops into the orange
    liquid,
gone forever.

But I've made it to the
    trapeze,
one of the easiest obstacles.
I slide my hands across
the skinny metal bar,
until my feet rest
on the final board at the end
    of the course,
and jump into soft sand.
I've made it.

I scoop up my fallen shoe
and head back to the house:
a successful adventure.
I have tamed the volcano.

Now,
on a bleak day in October,
the many fingers
on the end of the rake
dig into almost frozen earth
as I gather leaves
before the first snowfall.

Finally I reach the last section
    of the lawn,
the spot surrounding the
    swing set,
surrounding my memories of
    childhood.
But
when I glance back,
all I see are
the weeds that litter the
    sandbox,
one swing hung down
fallen from its hook,
the adventure and
    excitement gone,
the lava vanished,

and only a calm sea
of dark woodchips.

man. Because he writes, he notices what matters, he has thoughts and feelings about the world around him, and he captures them. His teachers expected that he would, showed him how, gave him time, and introduced him to authors and poets who demonstrated not only how to write, but *why*.

As a reader, Cameron finished thirty books during eighth grade. The titles represent nine genres: contemporary realistic fiction, memoir, journalism, fantasy, sci-fi, mystery, sports novel, antiwar novel, and poetry collection. Readers who are knowledgeable about young

As a seventh grader, Cam browses among the new titles

adult books will recognize Cam's choices as smart and literary—lots of well-reviewed titles, written by authors who know how to develop convincing characters, invent compelling problems for them, point a theme that matters, and spin a great tale.

Cam's two favorites of the year were *As Simple as Snow* by Gregory Galloway and *It's Kind of a Funny Story* by Ned Vizzini. In his final self-evaluation in reading, he wrote that Galloway "created an interesting, mysterious plot and included clues about the solution to the mystery, but not obvious ones, to keep a reader guessing and thinking throughout the story. Galloway created a believable setting, too, with life-like characters with unique personalities that I liked." In *It's Kind of a Funny Story*, he appreciated "strong, unforgettable characters; many thoughts and feelings of the main character, which allowed me to connect and bond with him; descriptive and sensory language that create strong, detailed visuals; an interesting plot; and a powerful and meaningful theme about figuring out who you really are and what you really want."

Cam also gave high marks to *Godless* and *Invisible* by Pete Hautman, *Memory Boy* by Will Weaver, M. T. Anderson's *Feed*, *Crunch Time* by Mariah Fredericks, *After* by Francine Prose, Carl Deuker's *High Heat*, *This Boy's Life* by Tobias Wolfe, *If I Die in a Combat Zone* by Tim O'Brien, Brent Runyon's *The Burn Journals*,

Prep by Jake Colburn, John Coy's *Crackback*, *Fallen Angels* by Walter Dean Myers, *In Cold Blood*, *The Catcher in the Rye*, *Johnny Got His Gun*, three novels by David Lubar, and *Here, Bullet*, Brian Turner's collection of poems about his Army experience in Iraq. Except for *Swallowing Stones* by Joyce McDonald and *The Brimstone Journals* by Ron Koertge, which earned 7s, he rated everything he read at least an 8 out of 10. He didn't abandon any books. He was, he said, "pretty confident already of every book I picked, that it was going to be good, because of the booktalks or what other kids had said about it."

Between October and June of eighth grade, Cam wrote a dozen letter-essays to me and his friends about his books. I think his response to *High Heat*, below, illustrates how the subject matter of the books available to boys is crucial. Cam could participate in and critique Deuker's writing about baseball, based on his own experiences on the mound.

9/25

Dear Nancie,

I have recently finished *High Heat* by Carl Deuker and thought it was an amazing, well-written sports novel, the best I have read of this genre.

I think Deuker did an excellent job of capturing the exact thoughts and feelings of a pitcher trying to close out a game. Because of this, being a pitcher myself, I could relate to Shane, the main character, when he was on the mound trying to close out the game.

I also think Deuker did a good job using correct baseball phrases and terminology. Here is a passage to show how well he does this:

I checked the runners, paused, then fired. I was trying to put the fastball right down the middle of the plate, but the pitch sailed inside. Reese jumped back and out of the way, his helmet coming off in the process. "Ball one!" the umpire cried, and from the Shorelake side I heard a chorus of boos. "Watch your pitches, Kid!" somebody yelled.

I took off my glove, rubbed up the baseball, and stepped back onto the pitching rubber. Gold put down one finger, but this time he set up the outside corner. I stretched, my eyes focused on his glove, and I delivered. Reese let it go by. "Strike one!" the umpire yelled.

Gold tossed the ball back to me. I looked in for the next sign, but I also watched Reese's feet. He didn't move up in the batter's box. Gold called for another fastball on the outside corner. Again, I stretched, checked the runners, delivered. My arm felt strong; the ball rocketed to home plate. "Strike two!" the umpire called.

"That was outside!" some parent on the Shorelake side yelled.

"One more strike!" Grandison called.

Reese stepped out of the batter's box, adjusted his batting gloves, then stepped back in. Only this time, he moved closer to home plate.

I knew what was going through his mind. He was hoping I'd lay another fastball on the outside corner. If I did, he would try to poke it into right field.

I looked in for the sign. Gold called for another fastball. I nodded, but I wasn't going outside this time. I'd set him up for the fastball inside, set him up to strike him out. So that's what I had to do. I went into my stretch, checked the runners, and delivered. The ball flew out of my hand: a letter-high fastball that painted the inside corner. Reese jumped back as if it were close to hitting him. For a long second the umpire said nothing. At last he brought up his hand. "Strike three!" (pp. 270–271).

I also think Deuker does a great job capturing the thoughts and feelings of a teen after his dad has committed suicide. He showed well how that affects their family, their own mental states, life style, etc.

I think that *H. H.* has an important and satisfying/concluding ending. I recommend this book to any baseball player or sports novel fan, and I rated it a 10.

Your friend,
Cameron B.

Cam has nothing in common with the main character of *Invisible*, a novel that's the subject of another of his letter-essays. This one shows him critiquing author Pete Hautman's narrative style, describing how he read the book, comparing it to another young adult novel, and still weighing in personally: this is what it felt like to read *Invisible*.

Dear Nancie,

I have recently finished the novel *Invisible* by Pete Hautman. I definitely rated it a 10, and I can't wait to read more of his books, like *Godless*, which I also enjoyed very much.

The first thing that stood out for me was how P. Hautman did an excellent job showing how precise, unique, and strange Doug's personality is, and how he's obsessed about his bridge, and also how he cherishes his scale model train village: Madham.

To demonstrate this I have chosen this passage: it's his English teacher talking to Doug about his essay, and the dialogue and thoughts and feelings show a lot about who Doug is.

" . . . if you were to write on a topic that was not so . . . *important* to you, your writing might in fact be clearer and more readable. As a related comment on your work, I'd like to remind you that when I ask for a three page essay, it is not necessary for you to turn in a thirty page dissertation."

"Some of those pages were drawings and photographs."

"Yes, well, even so, you must have had five thousand words in there."

"Four thousand nine hundred thirteen." That's seventeen cubed, but I don't bother pointing that out to Mr. Haughton. "You said that we could write a longer essay for extra credit."

"I did? Oh, well, perhaps I did . . . but in the future, Douglas . . . please consider another topic. That's all I'm saying."

As you can see, Mr. Haughton is not a clear-thinking individual. What he says actually makes little sense. Consider the following useful information that Mr. Haughton wanted me to cut out of my essay.

Total length of the bridge: 3.33 meters. Length of main span: 2.34 meters. Width of bridge: 7 cm. Clearance above water: 12 cm. Height of towers: 34 cm. Number of main cables: 2. Composition of main cables: braided ¼-inch nylon cord (orange). Number of stringers: 391. Composition of stringers: cotton string (dyed orange). Inches of thread used: 6,092 cm. Number of matchsticks used: 8,600. Paints used: semigloss enamel (International Orange) and matte enamel (Battleship Gray).

I might also mention that he is dead wrong when he says that writing and bridge building are the same thing. They are actually quite different. I know, because I am quite good at both of them (pp. 54-55).

I think this really shows what Dougie's personality is like and what he would be like as a real human being, how he is so obsessive.

Then I was completely surprised and shocked when I had read this, on page 116:

"'Douglas, Andy is not with us anymore. You know that.'

I glare at her. She is so wrong. She doesn't know how wrong she is.

"Andy Morrow died nearly three years ago, Douglas. You remember that, don't you?"

I close my eyes. The fire is hotter now.

"Douglas?"

"What?"

"Andy is dead."

I think (personally) it was the most shocking, most unexpected, and the largest twist I have seen in a book (even over *The Rag and Bone Shop* ending). And at the same time I thought it was a creative and a very powerful twist. I think I reread it two or three times to make sure it was really happening in the story.

In the end I thought this was a well written, amazing, moving book, and I recommend it to anybody who enjoys *any* type of realistic fiction. I think P. Hautman is a great and convincing author. What did you think of *Invisible* and its twist and conclusion?

Your friend,

Cameron B.

Cam borrowed *High Heat, Invisible,* and every other book he read in eighth grade from the classroom library. Most were volumes that classmates or I had booktalked. He jotted down each title that sounded good on the someday page in his notebook, so when he was ready for his next book, he could check his list

An eighth grader tells about a book he loves

of prospects. I personally recommended a handful of his titles, in the whispered conversations of reading workshop—*Memory Boy* and *If I Die in a Combat Zone* come to mind—and his friends Lincoln and Nate told him about *High Heat* and *Feed.* Cam read *Crackback* after I bought it with him in mind because of its subject, a high school football player pressured to use steroids. I asked if he wanted to preview the novel; he did, then rated it a 10 and booktalked it to the class. Like many of his guy friends, he located most of his reading choices on the classroom books-we-love display.

During his eighth-grade year, the boys in Cam's class read an average of forty books, with Cam at the low end and Nathaniel finishing sixty-nine titles. That's *a lot* of books, read—and talked about, traded, and fought over—with a lot of pleasure. Cameron and his friends had easy access to gripping stories with characters, problems, and themes that guys could respond to. These stories made reading an *active experience.* The boys adventured richly, within their imaginations and without stirring from the comfort of their beanbag chairs.

I separated the lists of book titles that appear on the Kids Recommend page on CTL's website into girls' choices and boys' choices because, in general, their tastes in books aren't the same—at the middle-school level, the overlap in titles is only about twenty percent. I'm a female English teacher, and as much as I love some of the young adult authors who girl readers are drawn to—Sarah Dessen, for one, is a genius—and as much as I appreciate Fitzgerald, Hemingway, Dickens, Steinbeck, and Twain, I'm responsible to help the guys I teach to discover the reading zone. This means they have to come to books on their terms, not mine. I can only encourage them if I'm intimate with the stories—imagined and true—that middle school boys will want to lose themselves in.

Then I pitch those books hard, individually and to the group, and invite kids to conduct booktalks, too. I show students how to keep a someday page to remember and follow up on titles that sound good to them. I make sure the books are easy to find, insist on time to read in class and at home, don't hinder readers with busywork or required genres, talk to them reader-to-reader, and convey nothing, ever, to anyone about book reading other than my certain knowledge that it is among the best of all reasons to be alive and human.

If you met Cameron and you asked him about me, as a teacher, I think *maybe* he'd say, "Yeah, she was pretty good." In the two years he was my student, I had a hard time getting him to make eye contact with me, and I can't remember that he ever initiated a conversation. His favorite subjects in middle school were math and phys ed. In short, as a reader, he wasn't performing for the teacher. Cam read to satisfy himself.

Among his strengths as a reader, which he described in his final self-evaluation, Cam noted, "I choose books that appeal to me and that I can engage in. I try and explore new authors, genres, and themes, which gives me a diverse group of books, so I find new characters, authors, and genres that I enjoy. I don't read a book that I dislike or can't engage with."

So here's a boy reader. He knows what he likes. He selects and rejects. He's tough-minded, curious, and intentional: he's looking for novelty, engagement, and vicarious experiences with characters, fictional and real, who interest him. He wants stories with guy characters. His reading habit is well established. He's fluent. He's critical. The only crisis confronting Cameron, now that he has matriculated to high school, is the ninth-grade English curriculum.

Along with all the other boys and girls whose teachers have barred the door to the reading zone, Cam is going to have to find his own way back in, without books and without time. After his graduation from CTL, he borrowed one of his someday titles from my classroom library—*Into Thin Air* by Jon Krakauer—but he never got to read it. His entire summer between eighth grade and ninth was consumed by the assigned novels of freshman English and twenty pages of double-entry journal notes about each of them, along with two critical essays. My fingers are crossed hard that someday he'll make it back into the reading zone, but my mind is boggled that everyone is so willing to leave it to chance.

CHAPTER 9

High School

A passionate reader—and soon-to-be ninth grader

Now, when I run into them, I've learned not to ask, "So, what are you reading?" Not the girl who read 124 books during eighth grade. Not the boy who read every dystopian science-fiction novel I could lay hands on, from *The House of the Scorpion* and *After*, to *Brave New World*, *A Clockwork Orange*, *1984*, and *The Handmaid's Tale*.

Not his friend who enrolled in CTL at age twelve, never having chosen or read a novel on his own, who graduated with sixty-four titles he loved under his belt. I don't ask them because most of the time I already know the answer, and it kills me: "Nothing. I can't. The assignments for freshman English eat all my time."

When they leave CTL, my students matriculate to a range of different high schools—local publics, local independents, and private boarding schools. Wherever they end up, most of them put pleasure reading on *pause* for four years, because they want to pass high school English. The sheer waste of time, not to mention opportunity, is beyond lamentable. Young adults are trying to make sense of adulthood—it is *really* just around the corner now—but their schools too often engage them in a version of reading that's so limiting *and* demanding, so bereft of intentionality or personal meaning, that what they learn is to forgo pleasure reading and its satisfactions and, for four years, "do English."

Some readers will find their way back to the zone, to frequent, voluminous experiences with books, after they graduate from high school. And in the meantime, a few—the lucky ones—will get their summers off; they'll never have to entirely abandon their identities as skilled, passionate, habitual, critical readers. When I tracked down some of the readers who graduated from CTL, to listen to what they have to say about reading in high school, their stories describe secondary English teachers who I *know* must have entered the profession for the same reason I did—because they love literature—but who've become enmeshed in a pedagogical paradigm that, in combination with a national standards movement, conspires to deny our secondary students easy, pleasurable access to books.

This chapter is a plea to my colleagues who are teaching in high schools. Please, for the sake of kids and books—and everything we know from NAEP and SAT scores, PISA results, you name it, about the highest achieving students—consider bucking the secondary English status quo. Every measure that looks at pleasure reading and its effects on student performance on standardized tests of reading ability—*and* science *and* math—tells us that the major predictor of academic success is the amount of time that a student spends reading. In fact, the top 5 percent of U.S. students read up to 144 times more than the kids in the bottom 5 percent.

As wedded as we become to curricula that we consider worthwhile and enjoy teaching—to the right books taught in the right way—we English teachers also need to think hard about the few and precious hours available to us to try to influence students for a lifetime. In terms of a typical high school English teacher's typical schedule—that's five fifty-minute classes per week—I think the crucial questions are *What's the best use of the brief time we've got?* and *What can we let go of, so we can focus on students becoming skilled, passionate, habitual, critical readers?*

Consider David. We spoke at the end of his freshman year of high school. As a seventh and eighth grader, he read seventy-five books. His preferences were contemporary realistic fiction, science fiction, and fantasy, and his favorite authors included a mix of young adult and popular authors: M. T. Anderson, Gordon Korman, Jonathan Stroud, Robert McCammon, David Sedaris, Dan Brown, and Michael Crichton. David listed his strengths as a reader in his final self-evaluation: "I love to read, and I recommend books I like to my classmates and listen to others' recommendations to find new books. I read many genres, and I read fast and with understanding. I abandon books that don't work for me. I'm reading more transitional and adult novels now. And I contribute insightfully and often in daily poetry discussions."

In my final evaluation of David, I described him as "joyfully literate." He was an opinionated, habitual reader who always had a book in progress and plans for the next one. His sharp insights in class discussions taught all of us, me included. And he was attracted to and appreciated big ideas and deep themes. His favorite poets were Billy Collins, e. e. cummings, Ted Kooser, Mary Oliver, and William Carlos Williams. In short, David was engaged, enthusiastic, witty, *literary*. It was exciting to contemplate what he would do next as a reader.

What he did next, in ninth grade, was to read six books: three assigned titles and three he chose from the teacher's list, which he was required to follow up with book reports. "You remember how I used to enjoy reading," he said. "Well, now I'm totally off it. We never get to read real books or even whole books—it's always one chapter or a short story for homework and then a quiz on it and a discussion. They never give you any time in class to read. There's no point to the book reports—you don't learn anything about the books or how to think about books. And then there's all the oral reports and the vocabulary, the grammar homework and tests, which also seem pretty pointless. How do I feel about English now? I guess you could pretty much say I hate it. The way they teach it, it feels like that's my only option." David is a conscientious student—he did the ninth-grade work, he earned his A's—but along the way the tasks of freshman English robbed reading of its pleasure and David of his "sense of purpose," as Alice phrased it.

Alice, an older CTL alum and, back then, an extraordinary reader whose favorite was Austen, finished more than two hundred titles during seventh and eighth grades. She stopped reading for pleasure in high school as she responded to the demands of an English curriculum that gave her no time to enjoy books and slammed the door on the reading zone. I'm going to quote her at greater length, because she was able to take a longer view. Alice looked back at high school from the perspective of her junior year at college, where she had just surprised herself by declaring a major in English:

> I was so busy with the summer reading and writing assignments, and the vocabulary, the grammar, the papers, oral reports, perfect notes, assigned novels, and all the stuff that high school English teachers give you to do, that I had to stop my own reading. I think a lot of it is that they don't know how to deal with smart, literary kids—the kids who like to read and write—and they feel they have to differentiate between regular and honors classes, so they establish a series of hoops for students to jump through. You've got to continuously prove you're one of the smart kids and that you "deserve" honors by performing this drudgery. Even when they broke down and let you "freely" choose a book, you still had to get the teacher to approve it first, and then you had to write a report on it.
>
> I missed reading so much. Every year, all through high school, I looked forward to winter break. For once, there wasn't homework then, and I could just read. It's the best feeling in the world, when you have a book you love so much that you just can't wait to get to it—not relax with TV or a movie or the computer, but read your book. I'd almost forget how good it felt, and then the happy, absorbed feeling would come back for two weeks every December.
>
> Now that I'm in college, I can read for pleasure in the summer again. Colleges don't assign summer reading, and even though I worked full-time, I finished more than thirty books last July and August, because I could come home from my job and relax with a book, instead of grit my teeth and get down to the summer assignment.

I don't do that much reading in my college coursework that's technically "free," but I do feel a sense of purpose to my reading. These are good books picked by the professors, not stuck into the curriculum by a committee. They read the books and loved them. When I'm deciding on my courses, I start by shopping at the campus bookstore—I look at the book selections a professor made and choose courses based partly on the titles on display that I want to read.

Looking back, as a reader, I'd say I became really smart about reading and literature during my time at CTL. Then I went to high school and got dumber for four years. Now, in college, I'm feeling smart again—literary and obsessed. It's exciting to be able to walk into a good bookstore and feel: *How can all this exist? I could keep reading forever.* I had forgotten how much I love books.

She had forgotten how much she loved books. This was the lesson Alice took away from high school English. And she was fortunate. She loved books going in, and she had a history as a reader to remember and return to. Students who don't enter high school as skilled, passionate, critical, habitual readers have an even slimmer chance of experiencing meaningful literacy, there or ever. Without memories of pleasure and satisfaction, without the level of fluency and skill that come only with frequent, voluminous experiences with books, they may never know the reading zone.

It doesn't have to be this way. High school English teachers can question the standard curriculum, and they can transform it. They can open it up to the needs and natures of secondary students and tantalize them with the independence, personal meaning, and sense of power that adolescents crave. They can sponsor the kind of pleasurable time-on-task with books that correlates with predictors of academic success. They can prepare students for what *really* happens in college English classes. And they can create and sustain generations of skilled, passionate, critical, habitual readers.

How does such a process begin? I think it starts when high school English teachers step outside the curriculum and think—and talk—about who they want students to be when they graduate: What kinds of readers? What kinds of writers?

What would your goals be for your students if you were to think of them as if they were your own children, then dream for them as a *literary parent* might?

I think I know one answer: their teachers would want every high school graduate to be able to read fluently, deeply, and with pleasure. The logical follow-up is *How?* Well, perhaps by trying to ease the way for students to read a lot and to love books. And maybe by putting frequent, sustained, pleasurable experiences with books at the heart—or at least as an essential part—of the secondary curriculum. Julie Lausé, a high school English teacher in New Orleans, did just that (2004).

Lausé describes four years of research she conducted as she taught a curriculum that combined independent, free-choice reading with a list of classics required by her English department. She started by assigning to every ninth and tenth grader homework reading of forty-five minutes a night, five nights a week, and also let them read during her Monday classes, which she established as a reading workshop. In a quest to improve her students' understanding, speed, and enthusiasm as readers, time with books became "the backbone of the English curriculum." Lausé distributed all the school's required readings at once, in September—in tenth-grade honors English, that was eight books—then assigned deadlines across the school year for the completion of each title, based on what she had determined as the speed of the slowest reader in the class. She and her students discussed each assigned book following its deadline, as a whole work, not in a chapter-by-chapter analysis, and she noted the "increased depth" of these literary conversations.

More significantly, each year, on top of the school's required novels, her students chose, read, and loved between fifteen and fifty additional titles of purely pleasurable reading. These ranged from *The Giver*, *The Princess Diaries*, Harry Potter, Ender's Game, and The Chronicles of Narnia series, *The Pelican Brief*, and *Rebecca* to *One Flew Over the Cuckoo's Nest*, *Catch-22*, all of Hemingway, *The Secret Life of Bees* and *Bee Season*, *The Godfather* and *The Prince*, *The Bluest Eye* and *Beloved*, *Great Expectations*, *Moby-Dick*, and *Persuasion*. Along the way, Lausé conducted booktalks, "put books into students' hands, and kept the dialogue going." She understood her role as a resource for her students—"a supportive cheerleader" for books, not a gatekeeper—if they were going to find reading easy and to read a lot.

Lausé's students changed, as readers and in their perceptions of reading. At the beginning of the year, only 35 percent of her ninth and tenth graders saw themselves as readers, and only 10 percent could articulate what made a book enjoyable. By May, she reported, fully 95 percent of her kids "see themselves as readers, have a clear sense of their reading tastes, *and* have a list of books they want to read." In terms of fluency, in September, 14 percent of ninth graders could get through only fifteen pages of text during a forty-five-minute reading session. In May, that number dropped to just 2 percent, while 72 percent of her kids were reading at least thirty pages per session, and 10 percent were reading more than fifty. With their teacher's support, high school students discovered the reading zone and recognized it as a worthwhile, stimulating place, one where they wanted to be.

Lausé, in her conclusion, speaks directly to other English teachers about her experience of teaching literature in a reading workshop: "We may feel a sense of loss as we move from being the center of the classroom to the periphery. But when students' reading and writing become the center of the class, their lives—and ours as teachers—are transformed." High school teachers who figure out how to invite and support frequent, engaged, voluminous experiences with books get to witness a dream come true: struggling readers turn into successful ones, strong readers stretch beyond the constraints of the syllabus, and all students begin to feel the same passion for books and reading that drew their teachers to the profession in the first place.

Selecting one's own books and having time to read them, in school and at home, aren't luxuries earned upon graduation, by virtue of surviving the curriculum. These are the wellsprings of student literacy, literary appreciation, and reading ability. Their teachers need to *expect and help* high school students to read a lot. In addition to choosing and reading good books during the school year, this includes pleasure reading during the summer, too.

My student Gina—a new graduate of CTL, voracious reader, and expressive, literary writer—matriculated to a small local high school, and promptly suffered the worst-case scenario of the summer-reading assignment from hell. In July, I spent an afternoon talking her down off the ceiling about the summer requirements of a ninth-grade honors English course labeled "Pre-AP."

By the end of the month, she was required to submit the following to her new teacher: a personal essay at least two typed pages in length on an assigned topic; at least ten pages, each, of double-entry journal notes about the three books she was directed to read, one of them *Cyrano de Bergerac*, of all things; and another two-page essay, this one researched with citations in the MLA format. Gina was beside herself—overwhelmed by the amount of work, angry that she had no time, for the first summer of her life, for reading in the zone, and already dreading and fearing her future as a student of English. She said, "The teacher wrote a description of what you have to do to get an A on the summer work. I'll never be able to do all this—I'll be lucky if I get a C. I used to think I was good at English and liked it, but now it's just a knot in my stomach." I think I understand her teacher's impulse—to bring rigor to honors English—but if we know that the students who perform to the highest standards as readers are those who spend the most time reading, why not clear the decks in the summer for as much joyful engagement with books as possible?

Other CTL alums, who went on to a local independent day school, reported that they're required to read three assigned novels over the summer, then show up in September ready to talk about them. As one student summed up her summer, pleasure-reading-wise, "At least I had July." Interestingly, the kids who won scholarships to the most prestigious prep schools, where I had expected they'd be assigned the most daunting summer tasks, reported the least demanding requirements of all: at Phillips Andover, one book, *The Grapes of Wrath*; but no specific reading assignments at Buckingham Browne & Nichols, St. Paul's, or Phillips Exeter, although BB&N does give kids a good list of recommended titles to consider as they decide what they'll read for summer pleasure. I asked Alison, a Phillips Exeter sophomore, why she thought this was the case. "Each teacher establishes his own curriculum at these schools," she said. "They can't give standardized summer assignments because they won't standardize a curriculum for freshmen or sophomores. The teachers get to use their judgment each year about the books they'll ask us to read, instead of having to stick to 'the freshman books' that some committee decided on." So, was she reading a lot for pleasure this summer? "Oh, yeah. Like a maniac."

A few years ago, a CTL parent whose graduating son was among the lucky ones—no assignment prior to the start of ninth grade—asked what I thought was the most productive use of his free time over the summer. I told her he should just continue to read for pleasure—at least half an hour a day, as he had during the school year—and to select books that interested him. She gestured to the classroom library and asked, "How does he choose without this?"

So I added lessons to reading workshop each June about how to continue to find good books, post-CTL, and I began to compile and publish on the school Web site—www.c-t-l.org—book lists for high school readers: pleasure reading possibilities, first for boys, because they have a harder time finding books on their own, then for girls, because it was only fair. After students leave eighth grade, they and their parents know they can tap the latest versions of the lists to discover some of the titles that are waiting for older adolescents. Although I came up with the initial titles, alums can contact our webmaster/school secretary when they find books they think former schoolmates should know about, and she adds them. If I were a high school teacher building a classroom library at the secondary level, these are the titles I'd start with.

One questionable practice that none of my former students has escaped, in English classes at every kind of high school, is the chapter-by-chapter reading and analysis of novels. Here, it's not so much the assigned nature of the reading that concerns me: I do recognize the benefits to older students when they spend some of their time as readers engaged with a smart adult around a significant—and age-appropriate—work of literature. What I find nonsensical is the ubiquitous chunk-at-a-time reading assignment, which undermines the integrity of a work of art and shatters the reading zone.

Imagine the impact on us if this were the way we had to endure another narrative art form, the movies. Instead of disappearing into the black cocoon of a theater, living inside a film, letting the experience of it settle within us, then formulating a response to the vision of its writer and director, what if we had to anticipate the approach of an authority figure who, every fifteen minutes, turned off the projector, threw up the houselights, gave us a quiz, and called on us to participate in a discussion of the movie so far? I don't think many of us would come to appreciate the emotional and intellectual power of a great visual story. I do think the effect of reading and talking about a novel in bits and pieces is similar. It just makes sense for English teachers to pass out the books, give students a set amount of time to read them on their own, give a just-the-facts quiz on the day of the deadline if they don't feel kids can be trusted to read a book without it, then engage in discussions about the whole work of art that an author intended and created, just as many of these students will in their college English classes.

And when secondary teachers do allow students to select their own titles, they might consider how pleasurable we adults would find our own pleasure reading if we were required to write something—a report, an essay, a journal entry—every time we finished a book. It *is* important for students to learn how to write as critics about their reading. But they do not need to write about everything they read. Here, too, I think students should learn how to select: Which books do they need to let settle inside themselves? Which are page-turners, about which there isn't a whole lot to say? And which do they want to think about more deeply and consider as works of art by writing about them? Daniel Pennac reminds teachers that while it can be useful to ask teenagers to respond to their reading, "it is not an end in itself. The end is the work. The book they hold in their hands. And the most important of their rights, when it comes to reading, is the right to remain silent" (1992).

If I were headed into a high school English classroom this fall—and anticipating the pressures of SATs, standardized tests at the state level, NCLB, and a schedule of 180 class periods in which to try to make a difference—I know I would want to think, hard, about my priorities: What do I give up because it's not an essential use of such a limited amount of time—or even because it might actually be a waste of kids' time? What do I keep—or add—because it will make a true difference for students as writers, readers, and scholars?

First of all, I would give up any packaged or commercial program. When it comes to reading and writing, there are no substitutes for time engaged in the real thing. I'd give up vocabulary study and grammar study, and while I was at it, I'd give up book reports, public speaking, oral reports, projects, dialectical or double-entry journals, and graded class notes. As far as I can determine, there's no correlation between any of these activities and achievement in writing or reading except for negative effects—for example, the time that grammar study takes away from students in their English classes has actually been shown to have a detrimental impact on their abilities as writers and speakers.

An eighth grader accustomed to, and expert at, choosing his own books

What would I keep, or add? At least one class period every week for book-talks and time for students to read books for pleasure—this in addition to nightly reading homework of at least half an hour, again of books that students chose. I'd make time for writing, with at least three English classes out of five reconfigured as writing workshops (Atwell, 1998), because students will require at least that much time to develop serious skills and habits as writers; here I'd focus on the genres that matter most at this age: poetry, memoirs and personal essays, literary criticism, and firsthand research. I'd teach either a reading or a writing mini-lesson every day, in which I'd introduce students to the processes, authors, genres, concepts, forms, and conventions that my current best-thinking determines are essential knowledge for smart writers and readers (Atwell, 2002). I'd devote the fifth day to discussions of common readings; I'd assign students to compose, as homework, a literary letter-essay every three weeks; and I'd sneak poetry into the curriculum at any and every opportunity (Atwell, 2006). The summer reading assignment would be to continue to read for pleasure, all summer long. I propose this syllabus with no illusions that it would be easy to pull off but with total conviction that it's a well-founded, authentic approach to inviting teenagers to experience adult-like literacy and become skilled, passionate, habitual, critical readers and writers.

Every September, when I return to my classroom as the teacher of a middle school writing and reading workshop, I get to remember and celebrate what drew me to the teaching of English in the first place. I became an English major in college because there, finally and fortunately, I discovered that I loved to read and that I loved literature. I became an English teacher because I couldn't imagine a better job than to nurture in young people a similar passion for books. I still can't.

L. S. Vygotsky, the Russian psycholinguist, wrote: "Children grow into the intellectual life around them" (1978). There couldn't be a healthier, sounder, more attractive, more stimulating version of adulthood to grow into than a secondary school experience that is filled with intriguing books, teachers who love them, time to read them, and friends to read them with. This is my question to the teachers who get my kids next: What is the nature of the intellectual life students will encounter in high school, when it comes to engaging with books? And this is my invitation: Wouldn't it be satisfying and stimulating, for them and for you, to teach so that every student, in answer to the question "What are you reading?" could respond, "The best book ever. Can I tell you about it?"

CHAPTER 10

Practicalities

*Circulating and conferring during
reading workshop*

Time

Every teacher I know feels con-
strained by time. Even at CTL,
where teachers determine the
schedule, we wrestle with the
limits of what it's possible to
accommodate within a seven-
and-a-half-hour school day. We
think and talk, often and always,
about *priorities*: a snack recess mid-
morning, so children can ingest
some fresh calories to burn; a
healthy noon recess—weather permitting, outside on the playground and field, otherwise in
the gym; time for art, music or drama, phys ed,
and Spanish every week; science and history
three times a week; writing at least four days a
week; and a math class and a reading workshop
every day.

So far, our best solution to the problem of the number of hours in a school day is a block schedule. The K–6 teachers carve out big chunks of time for a writing workshop and a reading workshop: from up to forty minutes each day for reading, then writing, in the all-day kindergarten, to almost an hour and a half for each subject in the grades 5–6 combination.

In seventh and eighth grades, time gets tighter, language-arts–wise, when we departmentalize and add a science teacher, a math teacher, and history classes to the mix. So I combine writing and reading in an eighty-five-minute language arts block, four days a week, and I break the block into five activities:

- Daily poem: 5–10 minutes (Atwell, 2006)

- Writing *or* reading mini-lesson: 5–15 minutes (Atwell, 1998; 2002)

- Independent writing and individual conferring: at least 30 minutes

- Booktalks/a read-aloud from the genre that we're studying in writing: 10 minutes

- Independent reading and individual conferring: 20 minutes

On Tuesdays and Thursdays, students take about five minutes for spelling studies (Atwell, 2002).

Dividing the block of time this way, into a series of related but distinct activities, accomplishes three things. It fits with what educators know about young adolescents' attention spans and their need to shift among learning tasks within a given time frame. It's predictable: my students can anticipate and plan for their engagement with specific books and particular pieces of writing. And it cuts to the chase by concentrating on what matters most in a language arts class: kids get to devote themselves to the work of writers and readers.

In my previous teaching position, I taught each class twice a day: one fifty-minute period for English, which I set up as a writing workshop, and a second labeled "reading instruction," which became a reading workshop. That worked, too. But I also know that although more middle and secondary schools are turning to block schedules, the single fifty-minute period, five days a week, is still the norm. If this were my teaching assignment, I'd get together with the colleagues who teach my kids and try to arrange a block schedule among us—for example, trade off short, single-period classes with the math teacher in order to create double periods twice a week for math and for a writing-reading workshop.

And if there were simply no way to shake extended chunks of time out of the system, I'd still establish, within the five short periods each week, a predictable, bedrock schedule, one that students could count on and plan for: three days of writing workshop each week, two days of reading workshop, and, for homework on seven nights, a half an hour of pleasure reading. I would allocate more in-class time to writing, as opposed to reading, because kids need at least three writing workshops a week if they're to grow as writers (Graves, 1983) and because students require more support when they're writing; they can read at home more productively than they can write at home. I'd teach a writing lesson on the days my students were writing. On reading workshop days, I'd plan mini-lessons related to books, authors, or reading, as well as a booktalk, or two or three, and I'd monitor the homework reading by multiplying by twenty the number of days since I'd last checked the page a student was on in his or her book. In other words, if kids had their last reading workshop on Monday, they should be at least 80 pages further along at the start of our next reading class on Friday.

Guidelines

Whatever the schedule—language arts block or single-period English—my goal for reading workshop would remain the same. This is a time and a place for students to behave as skilled, passionate, habitual, critical readers. Every September, during the first workshop of the school year, I distribute copies of and explain ten expectations for reading (see page 121). In a nutshell, this is what I think kids have to do in order to become skilled, passionate, habitual, critical readers.

Expectations for Reading this Year

- Read as much as you can, as joyfully as you can.

- Read at home for at least a half an hour every day, seven days a week.

- Find books, authors, subjects, themes, and genres that matter to you, your life, who you are now, and who you might become.

- Try new books, authors, subjects, purposes, and genres. Expand your knowledge, your experience, and your appreciation of literature.

- On the someday pages in your notebook, keep a running list of the titles and authors you'd like to try, especially in response to booktalks and recommendations.

- Write a letter-essay once every three weeks about what you noticed and appreciated about a book you've finished. Use writing to go back inside a book and consider the writing you read—how the book made you think and feel, what the author did, what worked, what needs more work.

- Recognize that there are different approaches to reading and different stances readers take in relation to different texts—for example, contemporary realistic fiction is different from a poem, which is different from a chapter in your history book, which is different from a newspaper editorial.

- Develop and articulate your own criteria for selecting and abandoning books.

- Each trimester, establish and work toward significant goals for yourself as a reader.

- In every reading workshop take a *deliberate stance* (Harwayne, 1992) toward engaging and responding with your whole heart and mind. Enter the reading zone and stretch your imagination, live other lives and learn about your own, find prose and poetry so well written it knocks you out, experience and understand problems and feelings you might never know, find stories that make you happy and feed your soul, consider how writers have written and why, acquire their knowledge, ask questions, escape, think, travel, ponder, laugh, cry, love, and grow up.

Then, throughout the school year, I teach so that kids can make good on my expectations. I follow up with support for individuals and the whole group, with time for them to read, with all the conditions for engaged reading that students named as essential to immersion in the zone in Chapter 2. The conditions are, in fact, a set of kid guidelines for their reading teacher—what *they* can expect from *me*.

Then, whether students read in class two days a week or five, reading teachers need to establish and stick with some basic rules that promote engagement and combat distraction. Ten guidelines direct my students' entry to and immersion in the reading zone. These appear on page 123.

CTL's teachers of grades K–6 adapted my guidelines for reading workshop to fit the developmental levels of their kids. Although the language and some of the specifics may change through the grades, the underlying principles remain the same: our rules and expectations define the school contexts in which children might act as readers, find sense and satisfaction in books, and enter the reading zone as early as they're able.

CTL students' record keeping of their reading is essentially the same, too, K–8. Every child has a reading folder that stays in the classroom, stored in a crate or file drawer, for the year. Inside each folder the teacher fastens multiple copies of a form on which students record the title of each book they choose, its author and genre, the date they finished or abandoned it, an overall rating of 1 to 10, and whether it was a Holiday (H), Just Right (JR), or Challenge (C). To help readers determine what genre a book might represent, Figure 10-1 (page 124) shows a master list of literary genres compiled by my students. They keep a copy of it, for reference, in a pocket of their reading folders. Our students' records of their reading are useful to them, to us as their teachers, and to their parents, as regular snapshots of children's progress as readers. And when it comes time for formal assessment, at the end of a trimester, individuals' reading records become essential data for evaluating growth and establishing goals.

Rules for Reading Workshop

1. You must read a book. Magazines and newspapers don't offer the extended chunks of prose you need to develop fluency. More important, they won't help you discover who you are as a reader of books.

2. Don't read a book you don't like. Don't waste time with a book you don't love, when there are so many great titles out there waiting for you—unless you've decided to finish it so you can criticize it. Do develop your own criteria and system for abandoning an unsatisfying read.

3. If you don't like your book, find another. Check out the books-we-love display. Check your list of someday books. Browse our shelves. Ask me or a friend for a recommendation.

4. It's more than all right to reread a book you love. This is something good readers do.

5. It's okay to skim or skip parts of a book if you get bored or stuck: good readers do this, too.

6. On the forms inside your reading folder, record the title of every book you finish or abandon, its genre and author, the date, and your rating, 1 to 10. Collect data about yourself as a reader, look for patterns, and take satisfaction in your accomplishments over time.

7. Understand that reading is thinking. Try to do nothing that distracts others from the reading zone: don't put your words into their brains as they're trying to escape into the worlds of words created by the authors of books they love. When you confer with me about your reading, use as soft a voice as I use when I talk to you: *whisper*.

8. Take care of our books. Sign out each book you borrow on your cards, then sign it back in *with me*—I'll draw a line through the title and initial the card—when you're ready to return it. Shelve the returned book in its section in our library, alphabetically by the author's name—or, if it's a book you loved, add it to the books-we-love collection.

9. Read the whole time.

10. Read as much as you can.

Genres . . . So Far

adventure/survival

alternative history

antiwar novel

autobiography

biography

classic

comic novel

contemporary realistic fiction

diary

dystopian science fiction

epic poem

epistolary novel

essay collection

family saga

fantasy

free-verse memoir

free-verse novel

gothic novel

graphic history or journalism

graphic novel

historical fiction

history

horror

humorous essays

instructional guide

journalism

law novel

legend

Manga

memoir

mystery: plot

mystery: psychological

mythology

new journalism

parody

philosophy

play

poetry anthology

poetry collection

punk fairy tale

retelling/recasting

romance

science

science fiction

series novel

short-story anthology

short-story collection

sports novel

spy novel

supernatural

techno-thriller

thriller

Western

FIGURE 10-1 *A student-generated list of book genres*

Assessment

When they read in a workshop, students are already in a constant state of evaluation: keeping records, choosing and rejecting, considering what is and isn't working in the texts they read, forming judgments, giving ratings, presenting booktalks, making plans, noticing their pace, monitoring their productivity, recognizing when they need help, and asking for it. So formal reading assessment at CTL begins with self-evaluation: the child's analysis of his or her work as a reader. We stop the workshop for a few days so kids can look back—note and reflect on accomplishments and progress—and also look ahead, to what they need or want to do next as readers. The process starts with a self-evaluation questionnaire (see page 126). Children write—or, in K–1, dictate—answers to questions about their preferences, literary criteria, accomplishments, progress, and goals.

Readers compiling portfolios of their criteria, accomplishments, and goals at the end of a trimester

Basic Questions for Self-Evaluating in Reading

- How many books did you finish this trimester?

- How many were Holidays, Just Rights, or Challenges?

- What genres are represented?

- Which book of the trimester was your favorite? Why—what did the author do in crafting it?

- What are your favorite genres to read these days?

- Which poems of the trimester were your favorites? Why—what did the poets do in crafting them?

- Who are your favorite authors these days? Why these writers?

- Who are your favorite poets?

- What was your favorite read-aloud?

- What progress did you make toward the reading goals we set at the end of last trimester?

- What are your goals for yourself as a reader for the coming trimester, in terms of:
    - your productivity and pace—the number of books next trimester or pages per night?

    - your work with genres and authors?

    - your written responses to books in your reading journal letters?

Depending on the focus of my reading and literature lessons in a given trimester, I've also included questions that ask readers to consider:

- What was your favorite memoir/short story/essay read-aloud? Why—what did the author do in crafting it?

- What are the six most important things you're able to do as a critic of and responder to prose literature—what can you notice, recognize, and react to?

- What's a book that took you by surprise this trimester?

- What will you take away from our study of the poetry of William Carlos Williams?

- What are the most important implications, for you, of our study of reading as a psycholinguistic process?

- How are the letter-essays working for you?

- What's something new that you tried as a reader, author-, genre-, or process-wise? How did it work out for you?

- In your experience so far, as a reader and writer of poems, what are the most important things you've discovered that poetry can do for you?

- What were your other breakthroughs or accomplishments as a reader this trimester? Think in terms of pace, experimentation, productivity, responding, choosing, and planning.

- Please finish this sentence in as many ways as you can: *I now realize the following things about myself as a reader:*

Every student also compiles a portfolio—three-ring binders that children fill with representative, captioned examples of their work across the disciplines—and presents it to parents and teacher in a student-led evaluation conference. Finally, teachers write our own comments about each student's progress: our perspectives, informed by the children's, on their accomplishments, strengths, and challenges across the academic disciplines, as well as final lists of goals, which are based on those that individuals generated in their self-evaluations, plus additions that the teacher deems essential. If a grade is being assigned, it is based on three factors: the progress a student made toward accomplishing the reading goals set at the end of the previous trimester; adherence to the rules and expectations of reading workshop; and the quality of thinking that shows up in the letter-essays. A long chapter in *In the Middle* (Atwell, 1998) is devoted to the minutiae of valuing and evaluating reading and setting goals and grades.

It may be more illuminating to look at one student—Meg, a reader who did not start out in the zone—and see how the assessment process helped her reach it. In the first trimester of seventh grade, Meg finished just eight books and abandoned seven. In November, when she drafted her reading goals for the second trimester, they were minimal: she wanted to read fifteen books, try a mystery and more Jerry Spinelli, and be more responsive to the questions that her correspondents asked of her when they replied to her letter-essays.

From my conversations with Meg that fall during reading workshop, I'd gleaned that many of the eight books she did finish were rereads. By October, her parents had already received two letters from me about her lack of home reading. I'd also observed the number of books Meg had abandoned, borrowed and not returned to the classroom library, or entered incompletely in her reading record. Just before Halloween she and I had a long talk about how she wasn't growing much as a reader yet, and I asked *why*. Meg said, "I just never learned how to engage in the zone. You might say I'm kind of lazy." I asked her if she were avoiding difficulty, or still not finding new books that would tug her into the zone. "A little of both," she admitted.

So I used assessment as an opportunity to nudge Meg in a healthy direction. To her three reading goals for the coming trimester, I added four more: read at least thirty minutes at home, *daily and religiously*; return CTL books and record books properly as she finishes them; abandon one book; and reread one book. It was time for Meg to become intentional. I shared the new goals with her and her parents at the November evaluation conference, and she copied them down on an index card, which she stapled to her reading folder as a visual reminder of what she was supposed to be working on over the coming months.

Then I concentrated on working with Meg to figure out the kinds of stories she liked best—fantasy, historical fiction, and light contemporary realism, it turned out—and to help her choose novels from among reliable alternatives that I pulled from the shelves for her—J. K. Rowling, Donna Jo Napoli, Kathryn Lasky, Art Spiegelman, Meg Cabot, Francesca Lia Block.

During the next trimester, Meg finished twenty-three books. In March, when she assessed her progress toward the second-trimester goals, she wrote: "I read 15 books, *and more*. I recorded books and returned them. I only abandoned one book!!! I read more than 30 minutes a day. I didn't accomplish trying a mystery or more Jerry Spinelli, but that's okay." Meg also noted that having goals, specific actions that pointed the way inside, "helped me enter the reading zone."

The assessment process helped both of us take a long view on what was happening with Meg as a reader—basically, it seemed to me, an unwillingness to engage the muscles of her imagination when it came to attempting and committing to unfamiliar stories and characters. A combination of personalized expectations that pushed her, and personalized advice that helped her meet the expectations, made it possible for Meg to be brave, to engage with a new crop of books that she loved, to grow as a reader, and to become immersed in the reading zone. Tom Romano has observed that "Our responses and grades should nurture" (1987). Assessment of their reading should focus on bringing kids along—on showing them specific steps to take to lead them into the reading zone, and on providing the support they'll need on the journey.

Communicating with Parents

Reading teachers need to work to build relationships with parents, too—to gather a team of adults who care about books and reading. A good way to start the process is by sharing information about *why* parents should care. The newsletter that appears on pages 130–135 goes home to every CTL family every fall. It explains why reading matters, what we do at school to teach reading, and how parents can help readers, especially young ones, at home. I invite like-minded faculty to reproduce it, send it home to the parents of their students, and begin a partnership with them as grown-ups who nurture readers.

Reading: How Parents Can Help

Everyone Has Reading Homework

The teachers at our school are committed to helping every boy and girl establish the habits of a reader and a lifelong love of books. Children leave school with one or more books to be read at home and returned to school the next day. The goal is at least a half an hour of home reading for every child every afternoon or evening. Depending on his or her age, your child may read to or with an adult or sibling, listen to the book read aloud, or read independently.

There is no more important homework than reading. Research shows that the highest achieving students are those who devote leisure time to reading, even when the school day and year are only mid-length and homework isn't excessive. Recently, the largest-ever international study of reading found that the single most important predictor of academic success is the amount of time children spend reading books, more important even than economic or social status. And one of the few predictors of high achievement in math and science is the amount of time children devote to pleasure reading.

Children read in order to become smarter about the world and how it works. They read to broaden their vocabularies and to become better readers —faster and more fluent, purposeful, engaged, critical, and satisfied. They read to stretch their imaginations, to escape to other lives, times, and places. And they read to become good people—knowledgeable about and compassionate toward the range of human experience.

There is no substitute for regular, sustained time with books. Please sit down with your child tonight and talk about the best time and place for reading to happen at your house. Is after school and before dinner a good point to catch his or her breath, curl up with a book, and escape into a great story? Or will your child join the book lovers who like to read ourselves to sleep at night? And whenever the reading happens, is the environment quiet? Is the TV off? And is there a good light?

We've learned that the choices of books available to kids today are so wonderful that reading makes for joyful homework. We've also seen that children whose parents and teachers expect and encourage them to read are likely to grow up as happy, skilled readers.

Tips for Parents of Beginning Readers

The following are suggestions for different ways that parents might support primary-grade (K–2) readers. These are enjoyable, successful approaches that teachers use here at school with our youngest students.

- Read aloud frequently from easy books that your child would like to read but can't, yet. Sit side by side, so you can look at the pages together. Point to words occasionally, and underline them with your finger as you read. Pause and make room for the child's predictions, questions, and comments about the story, the illustrations, and the language.

- Anticipate that your child will want to hear the same books again and again, and take advantage of his or her love of particular stories by trying to read them as many times as you're asked, even if inside you're groaning with boredom. Often these are among the first stories children will read on their own.

- Read aloud but leave an occasional blank, with your voice, when you come to words or phrases you think your child can guess at. Discuss the reasons for his or her predictions: clues such as the beginning letter sounds, the size and shape of the word, illustrations, and common sense within the structure of the sentence or the meaning of the story.

- Read a bit aloud—a phrase or sentence—while underlining the words with your finger. Then ask your child to read it back to you, like an echo, and underline it with his or her finger. Say, "Touch the words with your eyes" or "Read it with your finger."

- When a beginning reader is reciting a memorized book, ask him or her to "touch the words" as he or she says them, drawing your child's attention to left-to-right structures, letters, words, and the spaces between words. Say, "Read it with your finger." Ask questions: "Did it match? Did you have enough words? Did you run out?"

- Encourage a child who's beginning to read to select and reread books that he or she finds easy. In a bookstore or library, look for books like those your child brings home from school, with a strong match between the words and the accompanying illustration, and with just one sentence or phrase per page.

- Take turns: You read a sentence aloud, then your child does.

- Beginning readers sometimes substitute a word that doesn't make sense—or even sound like English. Try to bite your tongue and give them enough time to hear the miscue and correct it themselves. If they don't hear it, wait until the end, then gently question, "Did that make sense to you?" or "You read _____," repeating exactly what was read. "Does that sound right?" Then say, "Try it again, and think what might make sense."

- When your child is reading aloud with you and comes to a word he or she doesn't know, talk about its beginning sounds and its shape. Then tell your child, "Go back to the beginning of the sentence and get your mouth ready" to provide the word that begins with the letter[s] in question. Have him or her try the whole sentence again. It's wonderful how often children are able to put together all the clues—sentence structure, meaning of the sentence, letters, sounds, and shape—and read the correct word the next time through.

- If your child can't figure out a word or doesn't have a guess, by all means, go ahead and tell him or her.

- Encourage and praise a beginning reader's self-corrections and informed guesses.

- When your child wants to read a book aloud to you or someone else in the family, recognize that no one reads anything perfectly the first time through. This is called "miscuing," and although everybody does it, including parents and teachers, it can be particularly frustrating for beginning readers to make a lot of miscues. Encourage your child to practice alone first. Then, when he or she reads aloud the rehearsed materials, encourage phrasing and reading for meaning by saying, "Read it as if you're talking."

- Spend a short time hearing your child read aloud. Stop before he or she gets tired.

- Talk about books with your child just as you would chat with a friend: "What did you think of the book? How did it make you feel? What did you like? What didn't you like? Who was your favorite character? What was your favorite part? How would you compare it to other books about _____ or by _____?" Concentrate on your child's *feelings*, *preferences*, and *opinions* about the books he or she reads and the stories you read aloud.

- Try not to display anxiety or frustration. Lots of practice and relaxed, happy experiences with books are two keys to children's becoming fluent, joyful readers.

Three Kinds of Books

The books that children take home at night to read, or hear read aloud, fall into three categories of difficulty. Leslie Funkhouser, a teacher in New Hampshire, defined the distinctions we make among books here at school. *Holidays* are easy first reads or old favorites: a book a student has read many times before or one he or she picks up to take a break from harder books. *Just Rights* are new books that help a reader practice and gain experience—they contain a few words per page that the child doesn't know. *Challenges* are titles that a child would like to read independently but that are too difficult right now. There may be too many unfamiliar words, text that's too dense, paragraphs that are too long, a plot or structure that's difficult to follow, multiple main characters, or concepts that the child can't grasp yet.

We appreciate these definitions because they label books, not students. All readers of every age have our own Holidays, Just Rights, and Challenges. Often, as we learn more about a topic, work with a particular text, or just gain more experience as readers, a Challenge can become a Just Right. At school we watch as beginning readers make so much progress over the course of a year that a title they could only listen to in September becomes—over time and with practice—a book they read smoothly, with understanding and confidence, in June.

Children should spend some time at home with all three categories of books, but *most* of their time should be spent with Just Rights, because these are the books that help students learn the most, about reading and about the topics they want to read about.

Some time should be spent with Holidays, to help children gain confidence, increase their reading rate, revisit old friends, and read for pure pleasure.

Finally, children should spend a little time with Challenges, because these often tell stories or convey information that children want and can figure out with our help—and because they show students the books that are out there waiting for them as readers.

When your child reads—silently, to you, or with you—ask about the book: Is it a Holiday? A Just Right? A Challenge? If it's a Just Right or a Challenge, be ready to provide help with unfamiliar words or concepts. And, again, bear in mind that readers shouldn't spend all their time with just one kind of book. Children need experience with materials of varying degrees of difficulty if they are to grow to independence as readers and understand all the things that reading is good for.

Reading Aloud

Please don't ever consider your child too old to be read to. Here at school we read aloud to our students straight through graduation. Children of every age cherish the literary worlds that adults bring to life with our voices. The bonds of closeness that are created when a grown-up and a child enjoy a story together are one of the best things about being a parent, or having one. Strickland Gillilan's poem "The Reading Mother" ends with a stanza we think gets it right: family read-alouds are a treasure.

> You may have tangible wealth untold—
> caskets of jewels and coffers of gold.
> Richer than I you can never be.
> I had a mother who read to me.

When you read stories aloud to younger children, it will be helpful if you can select books from all three categories of difficulty, not just Challenges or chapter books. Feel free in your family to enjoy different kinds of stories and good writing, including picture books.

Final Thoughts

Your child may select an overnight book with content or themes that you question. While we know it's essential that children choose what they read, we also believe that your values matter. If a book bothers you and you feel strongly about it, ask your child not to bring it home, explain why, and talk with his or her teacher. The teachers have selected books for our libraries with many criteria in mind, from classic literature to predictable language and story structures to award-winning illustrations to cross-cultural themes to contemporary social issues. We're always happy to explain the merits we have found in a particular title, but we also want to support you if you have concerns about a book choice your child has made.

Because we use our collections of children's literature to teach reading, we count on the books being available to us each day. And because our trove of children's books represents a substantial investment of school funds and teachers' own money, we're discouraged when books disappear for weeks at a time or never reappear at all. Could you help us by checking each weekday morning that your child has a book to return, or continue to read, that day at school? And please scour your children's bedrooms from time to time for titles that belong to the school or to one of the teachers.

This newsletter about reading is, admittedly, lengthy. Reading is a priority activity at our school. We know that *nothing is more important to the development of children's abilities in every subject area than reading and being read to.*

From the first day of school, we make time for looking at books, listening to books, talking about the ideas and people in books, learning how to read books, and reading them. We offer students the most generous invitations we can devise to help them fall in love with books, see themselves as readers, spend significant time reading, and grow strong. We know that the richness of their early experiences as readers will serve them well their whole lifetimes, and we look forward to partnering with you as grown-ups who nurture readers.

A daily reading workshop in action

Three Kinds of Knowledge

When my seventh and eighth graders read Tom Newkirk's article (2000) about the reading state, then listed the conditions that make it possible for them to enter the reading zone (see Chapter 2), only one kid wrote anything along the lines of "Having a teacher who loves books." To tell you the truth, I was a little hurt. Here I was, demonstrating passion and commitment all over the place, and they hadn't even noticed. So I asked about it: Why did the class think just one student cited a book-loving teacher as an essential condition for engaged reading? What was I as a reader, wallpaper?

Jed spoke up. "Well, yeah, you are kind of like wallpaper. I guess we just take it for granted that our teachers love books." What I view as a baseline professional requirement, if a teacher's students are to engage as readers, is a given among the readers of CTL. When students grow up in a school where the teachers love books, often noisily, it becomes an assumption: reading teachers are grown-ups who live for the personal art of reading.

Each day I ground my teaching of reading in what I *know* as a practitioner of the personal art. I think about what books do in my own life, and what they can do for my students. I hope kids will want to apprentice themselves to me—trust that what I ask them to think about, talk about, and do will matter, make sense, and offer satisfaction. And I hope they'll take advantage of my experiences as a reader, just as I assimilate the knowledge of all my reading teachers, past and present, who have loved the personal art. In short, good teaching of reading begins not with the right method, system, strategy, or program, but with the wallpaper: what teachers know, and love, of books and kids. I think three kinds of teacher knowledge are at work when students become immersed in the reading zone.

1. The teacher's personal experience as a reader: our own encounters with books, as well as our reading about reading, books, and authors

If I'm to invite kids inside reading, I need to know the territory, not just as a reader of young adult novels, but of memoirs, short fiction, essays, journalism, poetry, and adult fiction, too. I also read *about* literature: book reviews, critical essays, and author biographies. And I read about teaching reading: Louise Rosenblatt and Frank Smith are my foundation, but also Shelley Harwayne,

Regie Routman, Linda Rief, Mary Ellen Giacobbe, Richard Allington, Marie Clay, Margaret Meek, Maureen Barbieri, Tom Newkirk, Jerry Harste, Jane Hansen, Ken and Yetta Goodman, Teri Lesesne, Don Gallo, Kylene Beers, Bob Probst, Alan Purves, Stephanie Harvey and Anne Goudvis, Janet Allen, Francis Spufford, and Daniel Pennac. To those who protest they have no time to read, Pennac says, "I've never had time to read. But no one ever kept me from finishing a novel I loved." Teachers need to grant ourselves the joys of good writing, and grant our students the knowledge we gain when we make time to read their books *and* to read about reading and teaching it.

2. The teacher's general knowledge of the needs, tastes, and obsessions of readers of this age—third graders, middle schoolers, high school sophomores, or whoever our students may be

The teaching questions I bring to my seventh- and eighth-grade workshop each year are pretty much the same: Who are middle schoolers? What are their concerns, tastes, strengths, and ambitions? Who's writing well for them these days? What are the books that will help them grow up—that will make them think, laugh, cry, and gasp, that will knock them out? What journals are reliable for reviews? Which bookstore collections are productive to browse? It's a big responsibility to build a classroom library and then continuously replenish the collection—keep it fresh, up-to-date, varied, and compelling. But without intriguing books close at hand, I don't see how students can enter the reading zone, let alone find a home there.

3. The teacher's specific knowledge of particular kids—of each student's preferences, strengths, and challenges as a reader

I need to forge relationships with my students that are centered around books: What is *this one* reading? Why, and how? How do I help her move forward? How do I support him as he builds a reading identity, so he can lay claim to his criteria and say, *These are my favorite books, the authors I love best, the genres I enjoy most, the poets whose works resonate for me. These are my rituals—the times and places I make in my life for reading. This is how I read a short story, a novel, a poem, a newspaper article, a scientific report, a difficult book, an easy one. This is when I speed up or slow down. This is when I decide to abandon a book, and this is when I stick with it, and this is when I cannot put one down. These are the ways I choose my books. These are the great books I've reread. And these are my plans—this is what I want to do next as a reader.*

The three kinds of knowledge of reading comprise my pedagogical money in the bank, accumulated over twenty years of workshops. I can never know everything about books, kids, or teaching reading, but I can continue to make deposits and grow smarter—more purposeful, more generous in my invitations to students, more responsive to what individual readers are trying to do, more aware of all the ways and reasons that people read, and, perhaps, less likely to buy into the "evangelical promotion of" new and improved approaches to teaching reading that are "misguided at best and simply profit-oriented at worst" (Allington, 2001).

Reading workshop is a great place for kids to practice comprehension, build fluency, acquire vocabulary, and develop critical, literary eyes and ears. But above all, it's the bridge. Children cross over it from the drabness of a world bereft of stories to one that's healthy, multidimensional, fully alive, delight-filled, and sustaining. The people and ideas they'll encounter here, the vicarious adventures they will live, can only be found in books. This is a reading teacher's best and lasting legacy. We were the ones who built the bridge and guided kids into the reading zone.

APPENDIX

How to Create a National Reading Zone

1. We need the professional organizations dedicated to reading—IRA and NCTE—to collaborate on a website of evidence that teachers can tap into in support of frequent, voluminous reading: research data and analyses that show its effects on NAEP and SAT scores, as well as other measures of achievement within and beyond the U.S.

2. We need the other state governments to learn from what New York is trying to do, and embrace reading standards that look at the number of books kids read each year and the amount of time set aside in a school day for children to read books.

3. We need private foundations that care about education to fund massive purchases of individual titles for K–12 classrooms, with the ultimate goal of at least 20 books per student.

4. We need state and federal governments to earmark funds for the purchase of books for public-school K–12 classrooms, with the ultimate goal, again, of at least 20 titles per student.

5. We need parents and teachers to lobby administrators and school boards to budget funds for teachers to purchase books for classroom libraries, rather than expensive basals and commercial reading programs that do not help children become skilled, passionate, habitual, critical readers.

6. We need administrators to make it easy for teachers to purchase books for their students one title at a time, with reimbursement and not out of their own pockets.

7. We need trade publishers to agree to give schools a healthy discount on books, that is, at least 30 percent off cover prices.

8. We need to acknowledge that school libraries and classroom libraries serve different functions; that kids need books readily available in their homes; that this is not a turf issue; and that school librarians can lend support to frequent,

voluminous reading through their knowledge of children's literature and by gathering and lending collections of books to classrooms.

9. We need a network of websites of great books nominated by K–12 student readers, from all kinds of school setttings, who know the reading zone: their favorite titles each year, as the go-to resource for selecting books for classroom libraries.

10. We need parents to band together, meet with high school English departments, and ask: Why can't kids be allowed and trusted to read for pleasure as their summer assignment? And, during the school year, where are the opportunities for our almost-adult children to choose books, discover their tastes and intentions, and develop lifelong reading habits?

11. We need to acknowledge that class is the issue that most impacts educational achievement in the U.S. How do we get enough great books for every student in every classroom—urban crowded and rural poor—and supply enough volumes of children's literature written in Spanish and other languages?

12. We need the whole community of people who care about literacy in the U.S. to ask of American classrooms: Where are the real books? Where is the time to read them?

REFERENCES

Allington, R. L. (2001). *What really matters for struggling readers.* New York: Addison Wesley Longman.

Anderson, M. T. (2004). *The game of sunken places.* New York: Scholastic.

Atwell, N. (1987; 1998). *In the middle* (rev. ed.). Portsmouth, NH: Heinemann.

Atwell, N. (2002). *Lessons that change writers.* Portsmouth, NH: Heinemann *First*hand.

Atwell, N. (2006). *Naming the world: A year of poems and lessons.* Portsmouth, NH: Heinemann *First*hand.

Berg, E. (1993). *Durable goods.* New York: Random House.

Caletti, D. (2005). *Wild roses.* New York: Simon & Schuster.

Carver, R. P. (1987). Should reading comprehension skills be taught? In J. E. Readance and R. S. Baldwin (Eds.), *Research in literacy: Thirty-sixth yearbook of the National Reading Conference.* Rochester, NY: National Reading Conference.

Carver, R. P. (2000). *The cause of high and low reading achievement.* Mahwah, NJ: Laurence Erlbaum Associates.

Clay, M. (1991). *Becoming literate: The construction of inner control.* Portsmouth, NH: Heinemann.

Davies, R. (1959). Battle cry for book lovers. *The Saturday Evening Post.* Expanded and reprinted in *A voice from the attic,* 1960. New York: Knopf.

Deuker, C. (2003). *High heat.* New York: Houghton Mifflin.

Galloway, G. (2005). *As simple as snow.* New York: G. P. Putnam's Sons.

Graves, D. (1983). *Writing: Teachers & children at work.* Portsmouth, NH: Heinemann.

Hakim, J. (1993). *A history of US.* New York: Oxford University Press.

Hansen, J. (1987). *When writers read.* Portsmouth, NH: Heinemann.

Harvey, S., & Goudvis, A. (2002). *Think non-fiction! Modeling reading and research.* Videocassette. Portland, ME: Stenhouse.

Harvey, S., & Goudvis, A. (2003). Reading and understanding nonfiction. In *Strategy instruction in action.* Videocassette. Portland, ME: Stenhouse.

Harwayne, S. (1992). *Lasting impressions: Weaving literature into the writing workshop.* Portsmouth, NH: Heinemann.

Hautman, P. (2005). *Invisible.* New York: Simon & Schuster.

Hinton, S. E. (1968). *The outsiders.* New York: Dell.

Jourard, S. M. (1971). *Self-disclosure: An experimental analysis of the transparent self.* New York: Wiley-Interscience.

Keene, E. O., & Zimmermann, S. (1997). *Mosaic of thought: Teaching comprehension in a reader's workshop.* Portsmouth, NH: Heinemann.

Kids and Family Reading Report. (2006, June). Commissioned by Scholastic; conducted by Yankelovich. Retrieved from www.scholastic.com/aboutscholastic/news/readingreport.htm

Konigsburg, E. L. (2000). *Silent to the bone.* New York: Atheneum.

Krashen, S. (2006). Three roles for reading for language minority students. In G. Garcia (Ed.), *English learners: Reaching the highest level of English proficiency.* Newark, DE: International Reading Association.

Lausé, J. (2004). Using reading workshop to inspire lifelong readers. *English Journal, 93*(5), 24–30.

Magill, F. N. (Ed.). (1991). *Masterpieces of world literature in digest form*. New York: HarperCollins.

Mead, S. (2006). The truth about boys and girls. Washington, DC: Education Sector.

Meek, M. (1982). *Learning to read*. London: Bodley Head.

Murphy, B. (Ed.). (1996). *Benét's reader's encyclopedia* (4th ed.). New York: HarperCollins.

Newkirk, T. (2000). Literacy and loneliness. *Ohio Journal of the English Language Arts*, Fall 2000, 18–21.

Pearson, P. D. (1985). Changing the face of reading comprehension instruction. *Reading Teacher, 38,* 724–737.

Pearson, P. D., Roehler, L. R., Dole, J. A., & Duffy, G. G. (1992). Developing expertise in reading comprehension. In J. Samuels & A. Farstrup (Eds.), *What research has to say about reading instruction* (2nd ed.). Newark, DE: International Reading Association.

Pennac, D. (1992). *Better than life*. York, ME: Stenhouse.

Pullman, P. (2005, January 22). Common sense has much to learn from moonshine. *The Guardian*.

Romano, T. (1987). *Clearing the way: Working with teenage writers*. Portsmouth, NH: Heinemann.

Rosenblatt, L. M. (1978; 1994). *The reader, the text, the poem: The transactional theory of the literary work* (rev. ed.). Carbondale, IL: Southern Illinois University Press.

Rosenblatt, L. M. (1980). What facts does this poem teach you? *Language Arts, 57,* 368–394.

Rosenblatt, L. M. (1938, 1983). *Literature as exploration* (4th ed.). New York: Modern Language Association.

Salinger, J. D. (1951). *The catcher in the rye*. Boston: Little, Brown.

Smith, F. (1983). *Essays into literacy*. Portsmouth, NH: Heinemann.

Smith, F. (1988). *Joining the literacy club: Further essays into education*. Portsmouth, NH: Heinemann.

Smith, F. *Reading without nonsense*. New York: Teachers College Press.

Smith, F. *Reading: FAQ*. Unpublished manuscript.

Sones, S. (1999). *Stop pretending: What happened when my big sister went crazy*. New York: HarperCollins.

Sones, S. (2001). *What my mother doesn't know*. New York: Simon & Schuster.

Sones, S. (2004). *One of those hideous books where the mother dies*. New York: Simon & Schuster.

Spufford, F. (2002). *The child that books built*. London: Faber and Faber.

Stafford, W. (1998). Notice what this poem is not doing. In *The way it is: New & selected poems*. St. Paul, MN: Greywolf Press.

Staton, J. (1980). Writing and counseling: Using a dialogue journal. *Language Arts, 57,* 514–518.

Suárez-Orozco, C., & Suárez-Orozco, M. M. (2001). *Children of immigration*. Cambridge, MA: Harvard University Press.

Veatch, J. (1968). *How to teach reading with children's books*. New York: Richard C. Owen Publishers.

Vizzini, N. (2006). *It's kind of a funny story*. New York: Hyperion.

Vygotsky, L. S. (1978). *Mind in society: The development of higher psychological processes*. Cambridge, MA: Harvard University Press.

Weaver, C. (1994). *Reading process and practice: From psycholinguistics to whole language* (2nd ed.). Portsmouth, NH: Heinemann.

Zusak, M. (2002). *I am the messenger*. New York: Knopf.

INDEX

A

abandoning books, 17, 27, 35,
128–129
"aesthetic" mode of reading,
42, 54–58, 64
Allington, Richard L., 138
Anderson, M. T., *The Game of
Sunken Place*, 84–86
assessment
basic questions for, 126–127
one reader's experience with,
128–129
portfolios, 127–128
Atwell, Nancie, 75, 78, 116, 119,
128
awards and citations for books,
noteworthy, 31–32

B

Baldwin, James, 48
beginning readers
teaching reading to, 41–42
tips for parents of, 131–133
Berg, Elizabeth, *Durable Goods*,
86–88
books
average number read annually
by students, 12
books-we-love collections,
36–37
free choice of, 12–14
levels of difficulty of, 40,
133–134
list of genres, 124
"page-turners" *vs.* literature,
18, 35
recommended by K–8 readers,
33, 104–105
selecting for classroom library,
31–33
teacher "intimacy" with, 33
bookbags, 38–39
booktalks
definition of, 66–68
categories of, 69–70
examples of, 70–73
boy readers
importance of book choice to,
96, 104–105
portrait of a, 96–105
stereotypes about, 18, 95

C

Carver, Ronald, 52–53, 61
censorship issues, 33–34, 134
Center for Teaching and Learning
(CTL), description of, 14–15
"challenge" books, 40, 61, 102,
133–134
checkout system for books, 38–39
classroom libraries
selecting books for, 31–33
checkout system for, 38–39
organizing books in, 37
Coffin, Helene, 41, 49, 89
comprehension, reading
as "recognition of meaning,"
60–61
"efferent" and "aesthetic"
modes, 42, 54–58
"relevant" and "irrelevant
bumps" during, 57–58
seven strategies of, as defined
by Pearson, *et al*, 51–54
conferences, reading
rationales for, 91
questions to ask in, 92
Cotta, Jill, 45–46

D

Davies, Robertson, 12, 15
DeMille, Ted, 41, 89
Deuker, Carl, *High Heat*, 100–101

E

"efferent" mode of reading, 42,
54–58
engaged reading, 22–25
expectations for reading workshop, 121

F

Funkhauser, Leslie, 40, 133

G

Gallo, Don, 31
genres, list of, 124
Gillilan, Strickland, "The Reading
Mother," 134
Graves, Donald, 73, 120

H

Hakim, Joy, *A History of US*,
61–62
Hansen, Jane, 40
Harvey, Stephanie & Goudvis,
Anne, 62–63

Harwayne, Shelley, 121
Hautman, Pete, *Invisible*, 101–103
high school
an alternative curriculum for
the teaching of English in,
115–116
difficulties of pleasure reading
during, 106–110
importance of pleasure reading
during, 107–108, 112, 117
one teacher's experience
encouraging pleasure
reading, 111–112
recommended pleasure reading
for students in, 114
typical summer reading
assignments, 112–114
typical methods of teaching
novels, 114–115
Hinton, S. E., *The Outsiders*, 33
"holiday" books, 40, 122,
133–134
homework, reading
nightly assignment, 24–25
rationale for not assigning
busywork, 39–40
Howells, William Dean, 27

I

International Reading Association
(IRA), 139
"irrelevant bumps" or distractions
from the reading zone, 57–58

J

Jourard, Sydney, 19
"just right" books, 40, 61, 122,
133–134

K

Keene, Ellyn O., & Zimmerman,
Susan, *Mosaic of Thought*, 59, 63
Kids and Family Reading Report,
73
Kids Recommend: webpage of
K–8 students' favorite books,
33, 104–105
Konigsburg, E. L. *Silent to the
Bone*, 56–58
Krashen, Stephen, 47